EDUCATION OF THE MARGINALIZED

EDUCATION OF THE MARGINALIZED

By

Dr. Ismail Thamarasseri
Associate Professor
School of Distance & Online Education
Mahatma Gandhi University
Kottayam, Kerala, India, Pin - 686560

&

Sreelekshmi M

Published by:

DISCOVERY PUBLISHING HOUSE
4383/4B, Ansari Road, Darya Ganj
New Delhi-110 002 (India)
Phone : +91-11-23279245; 23253475; 43596065
Mobile : +91 9811179893 / +91 9871656464
E-mail : discoverybooksindia@gmail.com
orderdphbooks@gmail.com
namitwasan9@gmail.com
web : www.discoverypublishinggroup.com

Education of the Marginalized

Authors: **Dr. Ismail Thamarasseri, Sreelekshmi M**

International Standard Book Number: **978-93-6224-668-4** (Hardback)

Printed at:
Infinity Imaging Systems
Delhi (INDIA)

Preface

Education plays a pivotal role in fostering equality, social justice, and empowerment in any democratic society. However, access to quality education remains an elusive goal for many marginalized communities across the globe, including in India. These groups—distinguished by socio-economic disadvantage, caste, gender, religion, disability, and geographic isolation—continue to face systemic barriers that hinder their educational and holistic development.

This book, *Education of the Marginalized*, seeks to explore the multifaceted nature of marginalization and its implications on educational access and outcomes. Drawing on sociological, policy-based, and constitutional perspectives, it presents a comprehensive understanding of how historical neglect and structural inequalities shape the educational experiences of marginalized groups.

The six units in this book are structured to provide both conceptual clarity and practical insights. The first unit introduces the concept of marginalization along with its socio-economic indicators. The second and third units examine the prevailing perspectives, policies, and persistent challenges faced by marginalized populations. The fourth unit highlights the constitutional guarantees and legal safeguards available to these communities, while the fifth unit focuses on strategies and initiatives aimed at their empowerment. The final unit outlines emerging research priorities in the field, offering directions for future scholarly inquiry and evidence-based policy formulation.

We hope this book serves as a valuable resource for students, educators, policymakers, and researchers committed to creating an inclusive and equitable educational environment. By deepening awareness and promoting informed dialogue, we aspire to contribute meaningfully to the collective effort of uplifting the voices and rights of the marginalized.

We are especially grateful to our colleagues, and the academic community for their invaluable contributions and support in the creation of this book. Our sincere thanks go to the faculty members and administrative staff of the School of Pedagogical Sciences, and School of Distance & Online Education,

Mahatma Gandhi University, for their unwavering support and the facilities provided during the course of our work. We are deeply thankful to our friends and colleagues for their emotional support and valuable ideas, which greatly contributed to the successful completion of this work. In preparing this book, we have referred to the works of numerous authors and information sources. We are indebted to these authors, editors, educationists, and scholars whose insights have been integrated into our text.Above all, we remain ever grateful to our parents, teachers, friends, and family members for their kind guidance and encouragement. We humbly seek God's blessings and are thankful for the strength and clarity bestowed upon us in completing this endeavour.Finally, we extend our sincere appreciation to M/s Discovery Publishing House, New Delhi, for willingly undertaking the publication of this book.

Dr. Ismail Thamarasseri

Sreelekshmi M

Contents

CHAPTER 1

Concept of Marginalization and its Socio-Economic Indices

INTRODUCTION

Marginalization is a significant social concern that affects the lives of millions across the world by denying them equal access to opportunities, resources, and rights. It involves the systematic exclusion of individuals or entire communities from participating fully in various aspects of public lifeeconomic, social, political, and cultural. This exclusion not only creates visible disparities in wealth and education but also undermines the fundamental principles of equity and justice.Marginalized individuals are often subjected to unequal treatment, discrimination, and neglect. These patterns are not merely accidental but rooted in long-standing social and historical structures that privilege some while oppressing others. In many societies, those who deviate from dominant normswhether in terms of caste, ethnicity, religion, language, gender, or abilityfind themselves on the fringes, unable to fully access the rights and services enjoyed by the mainstream population.

In India, marginalization is especially visible among certain groups who have historically been subjected to social exclusion. Scheduled Castes and Scheduled Tribes, for instance, have long faced social stigma and economic hardship due to caste-based discrimination and isolation. These communities often live in underdeveloped regions, have limited access to quality education and healthcare, and suffer from political under representation. Educationally backward communities and minorities whether linguistic, regional, cultural, or religiousare also affected. Their unique identities and needs are often overlooked in national policies and development agendas. In many cases, language and cultural differences contribute to misrepresentation, stereotyping, or even alienation from mainstream education and employment systems.

Women, children from rural and slum areas, and persons with special needs are other examples of groups facing multi-layered marginalization. Gender-based discrimination further intensifies the challenges women face in accessing education, employment, and leadership roles. Meanwhile, children in slums and remote areas frequently encounter poor infrastructure, low-quality education, and unsafe living conditions, affecting their development and future opportunities.Persons with special needs face both physical and social barriers. They are often excluded from schools, workplaces, and public spaces due to inadequate facilities and prevailing societal attitudes. This lack of inclusion not only violates their rights but also denies society the benefits of their contributions.Marginalized groups are typically identified using a range of indicators such as poverty, deprivation, and relative isolation. These indicators highlight the multiple forms of exclusion that individuals may experience. Other signs include systematic exploitation, educational backwardness, and persistent social inequality. These conditions are often intertwined, reinforcing cycles of exclusion and disadvantage.One of the most deeply embedded forms of marginalization in India is untouchability, a practice with historical roots in the caste system. Despite legal prohibitions, it continues to affect millions, perpetuating social segregation and discrimination in subtle yet harmful ways. Understanding and confronting such historical injustices is key to dismantling deeply ingrained social hierarchies.

Globally, several frameworks have been developed to combat marginalization and promote inclusive development. The Dakar Framework for Action (2000) emphasized education for all, especially for vulnerable groups. The Millennium Development Goals (MDGs) focused on reducing poverty, achieving gender equality, and promoting education. These were further expanded by the Sustainable Development Goals (SDGs), which prioritize inclusive education, economic growth, and reduced inequalities.India's National Education Policy (NEP) 2020 echoes these international commitments by promoting inclusive, equitable, and quality education. The policy introduces several progressive measures to uplift Socio-Economically Disadvantaged Groups (SEDGs), such as the establishment of Special Education Zones, the Gender Inclusion Fund, and reforms in curriculum and pedagogy. These steps reflect a growing recognition of the need to integrate marginalized groups into the nation's developmental framework.

MARGINALIZATION

Marginalization, also referred to as social exclusion, occurs when certain groups of people get denied access to areas of society. Many factors can lead to this denial of access to institutions and opportunities, including historical bias and lack of funding.That is Marginalization refers to the process through which individuals or groups are pushed to the edges of society, limiting their access to resources, rights, and opportunities. This can happen due to factors such as race, gender, socioeconomic status, disability, religion, or sexual orientation.Marginalized groups often face discrimination, exclusion, and reduced participation in political, economic, or social activities. For example, in education, students with learning disabilities may be marginalized if schools lack inclusive policies.

Marginalization is a multidimensional,multicausal, historical phenomenon. There are no general laws to understand and comprehend the complex nature of Marginalization. The analytical tools that can be used in most cases include class in relation to specific social, cultural, economic and political conditions as well as ideological systems. The nature of marginalization varies in different settings. For example, the marginalization of women in Arab is not the same as in India. Though they broadly share some feature. The religious, ideological system patriarchy, political economy of a country and the overall social system has its impact on the Marginalization of specific group or an individual. The idea of marginalization also varies in relation to elderly people living in Different countries and cultures. In some societies the elders are given more respect Compared to others. But it is opposite in some society because of this situation old people are subject of marginalization.Marginality deals with the socio cultural and human problems of people belonging to various sections of society such as Dalits, Black slaves, African, Americans, Native Americans, Pariah, other minorities such as Muslims and problems of females due to their peripheral place. Writers raise the voice in the different form of these marginalized groups. Whether they are Indian, Canadian, Caribbean, Indonesian or American. Words like centre and periphery have become so common that everyone is familiar with these terms.Marginalization is not a new phenomenon. In fact, it is as old as human race but the question has begun to attract greater attention only in our time especially with the advent of the post-colonial literature. The marginality is based on the binary opposition of centre and periphery writers who are at periphery try to occupy a marginal or borderline position.

Definition and Meaning of Marginalization

- **Merriam Webster:** "To relegate to an unimportant or powerless position within a society or group."
- **Robert. E. Park:** "A social phenomenon where individuals or groups are positioned at the margins of social, economic, or political spheres, inhibiting their access to resources and full participation in society."

- **Peter Leonard:** "Marginality as being outside the mainstream of productive activity."
- **Ghana. S.Gurung and Michael Kallmair:** "The concept of Marginality is generally, used to analyse socio-economic, political and cultural spheres, where disadvantaged people struggle to gain access to resources and full participation in social life. In other words, marginalized people might be socially, economically, politically and legally ignored, excluded or neglected and therefore vulnerable to live hood change."
- **The Encyclopaedia of Public Health:** "The process by which certain individuals or groups are pushed to the edges of society, limiting their access to resources, opportunities, and rights that are available to others."
- **Latin Observes:** "Marginality is so thoroughly demeaning for economic well-being,for human dignity as well as for physical security, marginal people can always be identified by the members of dominant society and will face irrevocable discrimination."
- **Sandra Harding and Nancy Hartsock:** "In feminist philosophy, Sandra Harding and Nancy Hartsock developed Standpoint theory, which highlights how marginalized groups, as outsiders within, possess unique perspectives that challenge dominant societal views. Their marginalization grants them an epistemic privilege, enabling them to see aspects of society that those in dominant positions may overlook.
- **Hall, Stevens, and Meleis:** "In 1994, Hall, Stevens and Meleis conceptualized Marginalization as a guiding concept for understanding diversity and social exclusion. They emphasized the risks, resilience and sociopolitical effects of Marginalization, particularly how dominant structures constrain and exclude certain groups from full participation in society."

These definitions show that marginalization is a complex, multi-dimensional process explored by various philosophers and theorists, each emphasizing exclusion, disadvantage, and the unique perspectives of those affected.The marginalized groups of people are observed all over the world. The marginalized literature is based on exploitation, agonies, pains and suffering, at the secondary level. The social, political, economic, geographical, special aspects of life which are deeply rooted in their consciousness with their past, present and future. Which are again present in the perpetually of time. Most of the marginalized groups, if not all constitute minorities, religious, ethnic, linguistics orotherwise in different countries, they have subcultures in this mainstream culture or religions.

Characteristics of the Marginalized Groups

Marginalized groups are often subjected to long-standing social, economic, and political disadvantages that result in their exclusion from mainstream society. They typically face systemic barriers such as unequal access to education, healthcare, housing, and employment. Discrimination whether based on race, ethnicity, gender, sexual orientation, disability, religion, or socio-economic statusis a defining factor in their marginalization. These groups are often underrepresented in government and other institutions, leading to a lack of policies and programs that address their specific needs and concerns.

In addition to institutional exclusion, marginalized individuals may suffer from cultural and social stigmatization, which reinforces negative stereotypes and fuels prejudice. They frequently lack a platform or voice in public discourse, making it difficult to challenge the status quo or advocate for their rights. This powerlessness can lead to feelings of alienation, helplessness, and mistrust toward institutions. Moreover, marginalized communities often have limited access to legal protection, making them more susceptible to exploitation, abuse, and violence.

Despite these challenges, many marginalized groups show resilience and maintain strong community networks, traditions, and identities. However, their efforts to improve their circumstances often face resistance from dominant social structures. Addressing the marginalization of these groups requires not only policy reform but also societal change through awareness, inclusion, and equity-based practices.

SCHEDULED CASTES (SC)

Scheduled Castes (SCs) in India represent one of the most historically marginalized and disadvantaged groups due to the rigid caste system. Characterized by centuries of social exclusion, they have faced systemic discrimination, including untouchability, restricted access to education, land, and public spaces, and limited participation in political and economic processes. Despite constitutional safeguards and affirmative action policies, many members of Scheduled Castes continue to experience poverty, illiteracy, and unemployment at disproportionately high rates. Social stigma and caste-based prejudices often persist, particularly in rural areas, affecting their self-esteem and integration into mainstream society. SCs are frequently underrepresented in higher-level professions and leadership roles, and they may also lack access to quality healthcare and housing. Additionally, Scheduled Caste women often face double discrimination based on both caste and gender, making them even more vulnerable. While efforts have been made to improve their status through reservations in education and employment, as well as legal protections, the deep-rooted nature of caste-based inequality continues to challenge true social inclusion for this group.

- **Historical Discrimination:** SCs have been subjected to centuries of caste-based exclusion, often forced into degrading occupations and denied access to basic human rights.
- **Social Exclusion:** They have traditionally been excluded from mainstream society, often segregated in housing, schools, and public facilities, especially in rural areas.
- **Economic Deprivation:** Many SCs live in poverty due to limited access to land, capital, and employment opportunities, making them economically vulnerable.
- **Educational Disadvantages:** SCs often have lower literacy and school enrolment rates due to systemic barriers, discrimination, and lack of access to quality education.
- **Untouchability Practices:** Although legally banned, practices of untouchability still persist in various forms, especially in traditional and conservative settings.
- **Underrepresentation:** SCs are underrepresented in decision-making positions in government, administration, and the private sector despite affirmative action policies.
- **Health Inequities:** SC communities often lack access to quality healthcare services, leading to higher rates of illness, malnutrition, and mortality.
- **Gender-Based Discrimination:** Scheduled Caste women face intersectional discrimination, suffering both caste- and gender-based violence and exclusion.
- **Lack of Political Power:** Despite reserved seats in legislatures, SCs often have limited real political influence due to dominance by upper caste structures and token representation.
- **Stigmatization and Stereotyping:** They are often subject to negative stereotypes and societal bias, which further reinforces their marginalization and limits upward mobility.

SCHEDULED TRIBES (ST)

Scheduled Tribes (STs) in India are among the most marginalized groups, characterized by distinct socio-cultural identities and a long history of isolation from mainstream society. They often inhabit remote and forested regions, which has contributed to their limited access to modern infrastructure, healthcare, and quality education. Scheduled Tribes frequently face land alienation, as their traditional rights to forests and natural resources have been undermined by development projects, industrialization, and deforestation. Despite constitutional protections and affirmative action, many ST communities continue to experience high levels of poverty, malnutrition, and unemployment. Language barriers and cultural differences further hinder their integration and representation in administrative, educational, and political systems. They also face systemic discrimination and are often stereotyped or overlooked in policy-making. Moreover, tribal women encounter multiple layers of discriminationdue to gender, poverty, and ethnicitymaking them especially vulnerable. Although Scheduled Tribes possess rich traditions, knowledge systems, and community-based living, their marginalization persists due to a lack of inclusive development and sustained neglect of their rights and needs.

- **Geographical Isolation:** STs often live in remote, forested, or hilly areas, which limits their access to infrastructure, education, and health services.
- **Distinct Cultural Identity:** They have unique languages, customs, traditions, and belief systems that set them apart from mainstream society.
- **Economic Backwardness:** Many STs rely on subsistence agriculture, forest produce, and manual labour, often facing poverty, low income, and limited livelihood options.
- **Low Literacy Rates:** Educational attainment among STs is generally lower than the national average due to lack of schools, language barriers, and social exclusion.
- **Land Alienation:** Despite legal protections, STs frequently lose their ancestral lands to industrial projects, mining, and deforestation, leading to displacement and exploitation.
- **Health Disparities:** Scheduled Tribes have limited access to healthcare, resulting in high rates of malnutrition, maternal and child mortality, and infectious diseases.
- **Political Underrepresentation:** Although there are reserved seats, STs are often underrepresented in policymaking and face challenges in voicing their concerns at the national level.
- **Cultural Marginalization:** Their traditional knowledge and practices are often undervalued or ignored in mainstream development and governance.
- **Gender Inequality:** Tribal women face triple discriminationdue to gender, poverty, and ethnicitymaking them more vulnerable to violence and exclusion.
- **Vulnerability to Exploitation:** STs are often exploited by moneylenders, middlemen, and contractors, particularly in the areas of land, labour, and forest resources.

EDUCATIONALLY BACKWARD GROUPS

Educationally backward groups are marginalized communities that face significant barriers to accessing quality education, leading to low literacy rates and poor academic performance.

These groups often include economically disadvantaged families, certain castes and tribes, linguistic minorities, rural populations, and womenespecially in conservative or traditional settings. Their backwardness is rooted in a lack of educational infrastructure, poverty, and social discrimination, which restrict their ability to attend and complete school. Many children from these groups are first-generation learners who struggle without academic support at home, and they may be forced into child labour or domestic responsibilities, particularly girls. Additionally, language barriers and cultural mismatches between home and school environments can hinder comprehension and participation. Limited awareness about the importance of education, coupled with economic pressures and systemic neglect, contributes to high dropout rates and low enrolment in higher education. The absence of role models, supportive policies, and inclusive teaching methods further isolates these groups from mainstream educational progress.

- **Limited Access to Education:** Educationally backward groups often live in rural or underserved areas with limited access to schools, teachers, and educational resources, making it difficult for children to attend school regularly.
- **Low Literacy Rates:** These groups typically exhibit lower literacy rates compared to the general population due to lack of educational opportunities and high dropout rates.
- **Economic Constraints:** Poverty is a major barrier, as many children from these groups must work to support their families, which hinders their ability to attend or focus on school.
- **Social Discrimination:** Members of educationally backward groups, especially those from marginalized castes, tribes, or minority communities, often face discrimination that limits their access to quality education.
- **Language Barriers:** Many students from these groups face challenges in understanding and communicating in the language of instruction, which is often different from their mother tongue, hindering learning and participation.
- **Gender Inequality:** Girls in educationally backward groups face additional barriers, such as societal expectations to perform domestic tasks, early marriage, and lack of safety, contributing to lower enrolment and higher dropout rates.

- **Poor Quality of Education:** Schools in these areas often suffer from inadequate infrastructure, poorly trained teachers, and limited teaching materials, resulting in substandard education.
- **High Dropout Rates:** Due to factors like poverty, lack of motivation, or the need to support their families, children from educationally backward groups often drop out of school before completing basic education.
- **Lack of Parental Support:** Many families in these groups are first-generation learners and may not have the educational background or resources to provide academic support at home.
- **Limited Awareness:** There is often limited awareness among these communities about the importance of education, leading to undervaluing or underinvesting in children's education.

MINORITIES (RELIGIOUS, LINGUISTIC, REGIONAL, CULTURAL)

Minorities whether religious, linguistic, regional, or culturalare often marginalized due to their smaller population size and distinct identities within a larger dominant society. These groups frequently face discrimination, prejudice, and exclusion in social, political, and economic spheres. Religious minorities may encounter restrictions on their practices or bias in public institutions, while linguistic minorities often struggle with limited access to education or government services in their native language, leading to cultural erosion and communication barriers. Regional minoritiessuch as those in remote or politically underrepresented areasmay lack basic infrastructure, employment opportunities, and representation in governance. Cultural minorities, including indigenous and traditional communities, often face the threat of assimilation, loss of heritage, and stereotyping. As a result, these groups experience lower literacy rates, limited economic mobility, and underrepresentation in media, politics, and public discourse. Despite constitutional protections in many countries, minorities continue to grapple with systemic inequalities and social exclusion that impact their identity, rights, and opportunities for advancement.

- **Identity-Based Discrimination:** Minorities often face bias and exclusion due to their religion, language, region, or cultural practices, leading to unequal treatment in society.
- **Limited Political Representation:** These groups are frequently underrepresented in political decision-making bodies, which affects their ability to influence laws and policies that impact them.
- **Cultural and Linguistic Suppression:** Minority languages and traditions may be ignored or devalued in mainstream education and media, risking the loss of cultural heritage.

- **Social Stereotyping:** Minorities are often subject to negative stereotypes and generalizations that fuel prejudice and social division.
- **Restricted Access to Education:** Language barriers, discrimination, or location-related disadvantages often limit minorities' access to quality education.
- **Economic Marginalization:** Minority groups frequently experience poverty and unemployment due to systemic exclusion from economic opportunities and resources.
- **Religious Intolerance:** Religious minorities may face violence, hate speech, or restrictions on their practices, places of worship, and religious expressions.
- **Geographic Isolation:** Some minority communities live in remote or politically neglected regions, resulting in poor infrastructure, healthcare, and public services.
- **Lack of Legal Awareness and Protection:** Many minorities are unaware of their legal rights or face barriers in accessing justice when rights are violated.
- **Vulnerability to Assimilation and Loss of Identity:** Dominant cultural forces often pressure minorities to assimilate, leading to erosion of their unique identities and traditional ways of life.

WOMEN

Women, as a marginalized group, often experience systemic discrimination and inequality across social, economic, political, and cultural spheres. Despite progress in legislation and policy, many women continue to face limited access to education, healthcare, employment, and decision-making roles. Gender-based violence, including domestic abuse, sexual harassment, and trafficking, remains a serious issue globally. Societal norms and patriarchal values often place women in subordinate roles, restricting their mobility, autonomy, and life choices. Economic marginalization is common, with women frequently engaged in unpaid or underpaid labour, lacking financial independence or ownership of resources. In rural and disadvantaged communities, these issues are compounded by poverty, caste, or ethnic identity, making women even more vulnerable. Moreover, underrepresentation in political and leadership roles diminishes their influence in policy-making processes. Cultural and traditional practices such as child marriage, dowry, and son preference further marginalize women from birth. Overall, women's marginalization is deeply embedded in social structures, requiring systemic reforms and empowerment strategies to ensure gender equality.

- **Limited Access to Education:** In many regions, girls face barriers to schooling due to poverty, cultural norms, or early marriage, resulting in lower literacy and educational attainment.
- **Economic Disempowerment:** Women are often concentrated in low-paying, informal jobs and lack access to credit, property, and financial decision-making, limiting economic independence.
- **Gender-Based Violence:** Women are disproportionately affected by domestic violence, sexual assault, trafficking, and other forms of abuse, which severely impact their physical and mental well-being.
- **Underrepresentation in Leadership:** Women are significantly underrepresented in politics, corporate leadership, and decision-making roles, which limits their influence on policies and governance.
- **Unequal Healthcare Access:** Gender bias in healthcare systems often results in women's health issues being neglected, especially in reproductive and maternal health.
- **Burden of Unpaid Work:** Women perform the majority of unpaid domestic and caregiving work, which is rarely recognized or compensated, limiting their participation in formal employment.
- **Cultural and Social Norms:** Patriarchal traditions and gender stereotypes restrict women's freedom, roles, and opportunities, reinforcing inequality from a young age.
- **Legal and Institutional Barriers:** In many countries, discriminatory laws and weak enforcement hinder women's rights related to inheritance, divorce, and protection from violence.
- **Intersectional Discrimination:** Women from marginalized castes, ethnicities, or rural areas face multiple layers of discrimination, intensifying their social and economic exclusion.
- **Reproductive Rights Limitations:** Women's autonomy over reproductive choices is often restricted by law or social pressure, affecting their health, education, and empowerment.

PERSONS WITH SPECIAL NEEDS

Persons with special needs, also referred to as individuals with disabilities, represent a marginalized group that often faces systemic exclusion and limited access to equal opportunities. Their marginalization stems from physical, sensory, intellectual, or developmental impairments that, when combined with societal barriers, restrict full participation in everyday life. These individuals frequently encounter obstacles in accessing quality education, employment, healthcare, and public services due to infrastructural inaccessibility, lack of inclusive policies, and social stigma. Many societies still perceive disability through a lens of charity or pity rather than empowerment and rights, leading to limited representation and voice in decision-making processes. Children with special needs may be excluded from mainstream schools or inadequately supported, while adults often struggle with discrimination in the labour market. Furthermore, public spaces and transportation systems are often not designed to accommodate diverse needs, reinforcing isolation. The absence of awareness, accessible communication methods, and inclusive technologies deepens this marginalization. To ensure their full inclusion, it is essential to adopt a rights-based approach that emphasizes dignity, independence, accessibility, and equal opportunity for persons with special needs.

- **Limited Access to Education:** Many persons with special needs face significant barriers to accessing quality education, such as a lack of inclusive schools, trained teachers, or appropriate learning resources.
- **Social Stigma and Discrimination:** Negative societal attitudes towards disability often lead to exclusion, bullying, and discrimination, both in social settings and public institutions.
- **Physical and Infrastructural Barriers:** Lack of accessibility in public spaces, transportation, and buildings makes it difficult for persons with special needs to participate in community life.
- **Economic Marginalization:** Persons with special needs often struggle to find employment due to discrimination or lack of suitable job opportunities, leading to higher rates of poverty.
- **Limited Healthcare Access:** Specialized healthcare and rehabilitation services may be inaccessible, inadequate, or unaffordable for persons with special needs, affecting their physical and mental well-being.
- **Dependency and Lack of Independence:** Many persons with disabilities face challenges in achieving full independence, whether in daily living tasks, mobility, or decision-making, due to lack of support systems or adaptive technology.
- **Underrepresentation in Media and Politics:** Persons with special needs are often underrepresented or misrepresented in media, politics, and leadership roles, which limits their voice and influence in society.
- **Lack of Awareness and Education:** Many communities lack awareness about disability rights, leading to ignorance and neglect of the needs of persons with disabilities, further deepening their marginalization.

- **Barriers to Family and Social Integration:** Social exclusion often impacts family dynamics, where parents may face stigma or lack support in raising a child with special needs, affecting the child's overall development.
- **Rehabilitation and Support Services:** Access to rehabilitation services, counselling, and social support systems are often limited, hindering the full integration and participation of persons with special needs in society.

CHILDREN FROM RURAL AREAS

Children from rural areas often face significant challenges that contribute to their marginalization, primarily due to limited access to resources and opportunities. These children are frequently located in regions with inadequate educational infrastructure, such as a shortage of schools, teachers, and learning materials. The quality of education in rural areas is often subpar, leading to high dropout rates and lower literacy levels compared to their urban counterparts. Additionally, many children in rural communities are expected to contribute to household chores or agricultural work, which takes time away from their education. Poverty is a major factor, as families in rural areas may not have the financial means to provide basic necessities, let alone invest in education or healthcare. Healthcare services are also often scarce, leading to malnutrition, untreated illnesses, and poor physical and mental development. Social and cultural norms may further restrict opportunities for children, particularly girls, who may face early marriage or limited educational opportunities.

Rural children also experience limited exposure to the broader social, economic, and cultural environments, reducing their opportunities for personal growth and professional advancement. This marginalization often perpetuates the cycle of poverty, leaving rural children with fewer prospects for a better future.

- **Limited Access to Quality Education:** Schools in rural areas often lack basic facilities, qualified teachers, and educational materials, leading to lower educational outcomes and higher dropout rates.
- **Higher Poverty Levels:** Many children in rural areas grow up in poverty, which affects their ability to access education, healthcare, and adequate nutrition, contributing to poor physical and cognitive development.
- **Child Labor:** Children from rural areas are often expected to assist in farming or household chores, which limits their time for schooling and personal development, perpetuating the cycle of poverty.

- **Gender Discrimination:** In many rural communities, girls may have fewer educational opportunities due to cultural norms that prioritize boys' education, leading to early marriage and limited career prospects for girls.
- **Limited Healthcare Access:** Healthcare facilities are often scarce in rural areas, leaving children vulnerable to malnutrition, preventable diseases, and lack of proper medical care, which hinders their overall development.
- **Social Isolation:** Children in rural areas may have limited access to extracurricular activities, socialization with peers, or exposure to different cultures and ideas, restricting their personal growth and broader social development.
- **Inadequate Infrastructure:** Rural areas often lack proper transportation, clean water, sanitation, and electricity, all of which directly impact children's living conditions and ability to study or participate in school activities.
- **Poor Nutrition:** Due to economic constraints, many children in rural areas suffer from malnutrition, which adversely affects their physical health, cognitive development, and school performance.
- **Cultural and Traditional Norms:** Some rural communities may enforce traditions or practices, such as early marriage for girls or caste-based discrimination, which prevent children from accessing opportunities or pursuing their dreams.
- **Lack of Exposure to Modern Technology:** Many rural children have limited access to digital devices or the internet, preventing them from developing digital literacy skills that are increasingly essential in the modern world.

SLUM CHILDREN

Children living in slums represent a significantly marginalized group, often growing up in environments marked by poverty, overcrowding, and inadequate access to basic services. These children typically live in makeshift or substandard housing with limited access to clean water, sanitation, electricity, and waste disposal systems, which exposes them to various health hazards and diseases. Education is often disrupted due to financial constraints, lack of nearby schools, or the need to support their families through labour. Slum children frequently face malnutrition and poor health due to unavailability of nutritious food and healthcare services. The social environment in slums can also be unsafe, with increased risks of abuse, exploitation, substance abuse, and violence. Many of these children do not have birth certificates or identity documents, which limits their access to social welfare schemes and public services. Social stigma and discrimination further isolate them, reducing their chances of upward mobility. Without intervention, these conditions severely hinder their cognitive, emotional, and physical development, perpetuating the cycle of poverty and exclusion. Comprehensive support in education, healthcare, nutrition, and social protection is essential to improve their quality of life and future prospects.

- **Poor Living Conditions:** Slum children often live in overcrowded, unhygienic, and unsafe housing made of temporary materials, which exposes them to health and safety risks.
- **Lack of Access to Clean Water and Sanitation:** These children typically face inadequate sanitation facilities and limited access to clean drinking water, increasing the risk of waterborne diseases.
- **Limited Educational Opportunities:** Many slum children have irregular or no access to formal education due to poverty, lack of nearby schools, or the need to work and support their families.
- **High Incidence of Child Labor:** Economic hardship forces many children to work in informal sectors such as rag-picking, vending, or domestic work, compromising their health and education.
- **Malnutrition and Poor Health:** Due to food insecurity and limited healthcare services, slum children often suffer from undernutrition, stunted growth, and frequent illnesses.
- **Exposure to Abuse and Exploitation:** Slum environments can be unsafe, with children being vulnerable to physical, emotional, and sexual abuse, as well as trafficking and neglect.
- **Lack of Legal Identity:** Many slum children lack birth certificates or official identity documents, preventing access to schooling, healthcare, and government welfare schemes.
- **Insecurity and Instability:** Families living in slums often face eviction threats and unstable housing, leading to frequent relocation, which disrupts children's education and sense of security.
- **Social Stigma and Exclusion:** Slum children are often discriminated against by mainstream society, facing social exclusion, which limits their opportunities for growth and participation.
- **Limited Access to Recreation and Safe Spaces:** The absence of playgrounds or safe public areas deprives children of opportunities for play, recreation, and social interaction essential for their overall development.

INDICATORS USED FOR IDENTIFYING MARGINALIZED GROUPS

Marginalized groups are those systematically excluded from full participation in society, and they can be identified through a variety of interrelated indicators. Poverty is a primary indicator, as it restricts access to essential services such as education, healthcare, housing, and nutrition, perpetuating cycles of disadvantage. Relative isolation, often geographical in nature, separates certain communities from mainstream development, information, and opportunities, especially those in remote or rural regions. Deprivation, both material and social, limits individuals' ability to achieve a standard quality of life and access resources necessary for advancement. Exploitation, in forms such as child labour, unfair wages, or bonded labour, highlights systemic injustice and power imbalances. Discrimination on the basis of caste, ethnicity, gender, religion, or disability further entrenches marginalization by promoting exclusion and unequal treatment. These indicators are not standalone but interlinked, often reinforcing one another and creating deep-rooted structures of exclusion.

Other crucial indicators include educational backwardness, where communities have significantly lower literacy rates and limited access to quality schooling, resulting in limited economic mobility and political representation. Inequality, both in opportunity and outcome, is another key marker whether in terms of income, representation in governance, or access to technology and information. Untouchability, a form of caste-based discrimination with deep historical and social roots in some societies, especially in South Asia, remains a severe indicator of social exclusion. The historical oppression of specific groups, such as Dalits, indigenous peoples, or minority religious communities, has embedded a structural disadvantage that persists despite legal reforms. Understanding and addressing these indicators is essential for inclusive policymaking, social justice, and equitable development. Identifying marginalized groups through these lenses helps governments and organizations implement targeted interventions that promote empowerment and integration.

POVERTY

Poverty is one of the most visible and measurable indicators of marginalization. It reflects the inability of individuals or groups to access basic necessities such as food, clothing, shelter, healthcare, and education. Marginalized groups often experience chronic poverty due to systemic exclusion from economic opportunities and social development. This lack of financial resources reinforces a cycle of deprivation and dependence, making it difficult to improve their socio-economic status.

- Lack of financial resources and basic needs (food, shelter, clothing).
- Limited access to healthcare, education, and employment.
- High dependency on informal or subsistence economy.

RELATIVE ISOLATION

Relative isolation refers to the physical, cultural, or social separation of certain communities from mainstream society. Many tribal populations and rural communities live in geographically remote areas, limiting their access to essential services like education, healthcare, and employment. Cultural and linguistic differences further deepen their isolation, making integration into the wider society challenging. This separation hinders their participation in development processes and perpetuates marginalization.

- Geographical remoteness (e.g., tribal populations in forests or hills).
- Limited interaction with mainstream society and institutions.
- Restricted access to government schemes and social services.

DEPRIVATION

Deprivation occurs when individuals or groups are denied access to resources and services necessary for a dignified life. This includes material deprivation (such as lack of food or shelter) and social deprivation (such as lack of education, healthcare, or justice). Marginalized groups are often deprived of equal opportunities and basic rights due to long-standing structural inequalities. This systemic neglect leads to poor health outcomes, unemployment, and low levels of human development.

- Denial of access to education, employment, housing, and justice.
- Often measured in terms of material well-being, literacy, and access to infrastructure.

EXPLOITATION

Exploitation is a condition where marginalized individuals are subjected to unfair treatment, often for economic or social gain. It includes child labour, bonded labour, and underpaid or unpaid work. Women, children, and lower-caste individuals are particularly vulnerable to such exploitation. Often, these groups lack the power or resources to resist or challenge exploitation, which keeps them trapped in cycles of dependency and poverty.

- Unequal power dynamics, especially in labour (e.g., bonded labour, child labour).
- Economic, social, or sexual exploitation of vulnerable groups.

DISCRIMINATION

Discrimination involves unjust treatment based on identity markers like caste, religion, gender, disability, or ethnicity. It is both a cause and consequence of marginalization. Discriminated individuals may be denied employment, education, or access to public spaces and institutions. Despite legal protections, social stigma and bias continue to affect the lives of marginalized people, limiting their opportunities and reinforcing their social exclusion.

- Social exclusion based on caste, gender, religion, disability, etc.
- Denial of equal treatment and opportunities in law, policy, and daily life.

EDUCATIONAL BACKWARDNESS

Educational backwardness is a key indicator of marginalization, marked by low literacy rates, poor school attendance, and high dropout rates among disadvantaged groups. Contributing factors include poverty, cultural barriers, lack of infrastructure, and curriculum that doesn't reflect the needs of marginalized communities. Without access to quality and inclusive education, these groups struggle to break out of cycles of poverty and inequality.

- Low literacy and high dropout rates.
- Poor access to quality and inclusive education.
- Cultural and linguistic gaps in mainstream curriculum.

INEQUALITY

Inequality reflects the unequal distribution of resources, opportunities, and rights in society. Marginalized groups often face multiple forms of inequalityeconomic, social, and political. For example, they may earn less, own fewer assets, and have limited political representation. These inequalities are often institutionalized and perpetuated over generations, deepening the marginalization experienced by certain communities.

- Structural and systemic inequalities in income, land ownership, and political representation.
- Reinforced by social norms, policies, and historical injustices.

UNTOUCHABILITY – HISTORICAL AND SOCIAL ROOTS

Untouchability is a deeply entrenched form of caste-based discrimination rooted in the traditional Hindu caste system. Historically, Dalits (formerly known as untouchables) were considered "impure" and excluded from mainstream society. They were assigned menial tasks and denied access to temples, schools, and community spaces. Though untouchability was abolished under Article 17 of the Indian Constitution, its practice still exists in subtle and overt forms, especially in rural India. The social stigma, violence, and exclusion associated with untouchability reflect the enduring legacy of caste oppression. Untouchability is rooted in the ancient caste system, particularly in Hindu society, where social hierarchy placed "Dalits" (formerly called "untouchables") at the bottom. They were considered "impure" and were barred from temples, schools, and public facilities.It was maintained through strict social rules, religious justification, and social conditioning. Dalits were confined to menial jobs (e.g., cleaning, leather work) and lived in segregated areas.Although legally abolished by the Indian Constitution (Article 17), untouchability persists in various forms of social exclusion and discrimination, especially in rural areas.

INTERNATIONAL PERSPECTIVES ON ADDRESSING MARGINALIZATION

The Dakar Framework for Action (2000), adopted at the World Education Forum, placed a strong emphasis on "Education for All" (EFA), with a commitment to ensure equitable access to quality education for marginalized populations. It identified groups such as girls, children in conflict zones, ethnic minorities, and those with disabilities as needing targeted attention. The framework underscored the urgency of eliminating gender disparities and reducing inequalities in access and outcomes. It called upon all nations to address systemic barriers including poverty, discrimination, and social exclusion that prevent marginalized children and adults from benefiting from education. Importantly, the Dakar Goals promoted a rights-based approach, focusing on inclusive, lifelong learning as a fundamental human right and an essential foundation for sustainable development.

Building on this vision, the Millennium Development Goals (2000-2015) introduced a global agenda to tackle extreme poverty, improve health and education, and promote gender equality. Goal 2 aimed at achieving universal primary education, and Goal 3 focused on promoting gender equality and empowering women. While the MDGs led to significant global improvements, particularly in access to primary education, critics noted that they often prioritized aggregate targets over equity, unintentionally neglecting the most marginalized populations. In response, the Sustainable Development Goals (SDGs), launched in 2015, adopted a more inclusive and comprehensive framework. SDG 4, which targets inclusive and equitable quality education and lifelong learning opportunities, emphasizes reaching disadvantaged groups, reducing inequality, and promoting education that is accessible to all, regardless of socio-economic status, disability, or cultural background.

In alignment with these global efforts, India's National Education Policy (NEP) 2020 embraces an inclusive, equitable, and flexible educational framework that echoes the SDGs. The policy envisions universal access to education at all levels, aiming to reduce dropout rates and ensure participation of marginalized groups such as socio-economically disadvantaged groups (SEDGs), including SCs, STs, OBCs, girls, and children with disabilities. It emphasizes the need for gender inclusion funds, scholarships, and infrastructural support in underprivileged regions. NEP 2020 also acknowledges the significance of mother tongue-based instruction, special education zones, and community participation to bridge educational gaps. By integrating international goals with local realities, the NEP 2020 seeks to dismantle historical barriers and transform the Indian education system into a truly inclusive space for all learners.

DAKAR FRAMEWORK FOR ACTION (2000)

The Dakar Framework for Action, adopted at the World Education Forum in 2000, reaffirmed the global commitment to achieving Education for All (EFA) by 2015. It emphasized inclusive and equitable access to quality education, especially for marginalized and disadvantaged groups including girls, children in difficult circumstances, and those belonging to ethnic minorities. The framework laid out six key goals, such as expanding early childhood care, improving adult literacy, and eliminating gender disparities in education. A core principle of the Dakar declaration was that no child should be denied access to education due to poverty, gender, disability, or social background.

MILLENNIUM DEVELOPMENT GOALS (MDG)

Launched by the United Nations in 2000, the Millennium Development Goals (MDGs) comprised eight goals to be achieved by 2015, with several directly addressing the issues faced by marginalized groups. Goals such as achieving universal primary education (Goal 2), promoting gender equality (Goal 3), and eradicating extreme poverty and hunger (Goal 1) aimed to uplift vulnerable populations and improve their access to fundamental human rights. Although significant progress was made in areas like school enrolment, the MDGs were critiqued for being overly focused on averages, which often masked persistent disparities among marginalized communities.

SUSTAINABLE DEVELOPMENT GOALS (SDG)

The Sustainable Development Goals (SDGs), adopted in 2015 as the successor to the MDGs, consist of 17 goals to be achieved by 2030. Unlike the MDGs, the SDGs are more comprehensive and emphasize inclusion and equity across all goals. Key goals relevant to marginalized groups include Goal 4 (Quality Education), Goal 5 (Gender Equality), Goal 10 (Reduced Inequalities), and Goal 1 (No Poverty). The SDGs explicitly call for leaving no one behind and focus on dismantling barriers faced by disadvantaged groups including women, persons with disabilities, indigenous peoples, and children in vulnerable situations.

VISION IN NATIONAL EDUCATION POLICY (NEP) 2020

India's National Education Policy (NEP) 2020 embodies the global vision of inclusive and equitable education by recognizing the diverse needs of learners and aiming to eliminate disparities in access. The policy prioritizes the education of socio-economically disadvantaged groups (SEDGs), including Scheduled Castes, Scheduled Tribes, minorities, girls, and persons with disabilities. NEP 2020 outlines specific interventions such as the establishment of Gender-Inclusion Funds, Special Education Zones, and the integration of vocational and foundational skills. It promotes a flexible, multidisciplinary education system that is inclusive in pedagogy and accessible in structure, aligning with the SDGs' broader global goals.

CONCLUSION

Marginalization continues to be a pressing social issue that affects the holistic development of societies around the world. It entails the exclusion of individuals or groups from full participation in social, political, cultural, and economic life, thereby restricting their access to fundamental rights and services. Understanding and addressing marginalization is crucial for achieving social equity, justice, and national development.The consequences of marginalization are far-reaching and often intergenerational. When communities are excluded from education, employment, and decision-making, it leads to persistent poverty and social unrest. These disparities widen over time, making it harder for marginalized populations to break free from the cycle of disadvantage. Addressing these issues is essential to building a resilient and inclusive society.

In India, marginalization is prominently seen among groups such as Scheduled Castes, Scheduled Tribes, and educationally backward communities. These groups have historically faced systemic discrimination that has affected their access to resources, representation, and dignity. Despite constitutional safeguards, many of them continue to experience social exclusion, especially in rural and underdeveloped areas.Minorities, whether defined by language, religion, culture, or region, face challenges related to identity, recognition, and inclusion. These challenges are compounded when minority communities are economically disadvantaged or geographically isolated. Women, too, remain one of the most marginalized groups due to entrenched gender norms that limit their freedom and potential in every sphere of life.Children from rural and slum areas often grow up in environments that lack basic infrastructure, quality education, and healthcare. As a result, they start life at a significant disadvantage. Persons with special needs encounter physical, social, and institutional barriers that prevent them from accessing equitable opportunities in education, employment, and public life.

Identifying marginalized groups involves analysing indicators such as poverty, social isolation, deprivation, discrimination, and educational backwardness. These indicators offer insight into the lived realities of affected communities and guide the formulation of targeted interventions. The legacy of untouchability, though officially abolished, continues to cast a shadow on the lives of millions, underscoring the need for sustained social reform.Efforts to tackle marginalization must go beyond policy rhetoric and address the structural roots of exclusion. There must be a focus on inclusive development, where the voices and needs of the marginalized are at the centre of planning and implementation. This requires strong institutional frameworks, political commitment, and continuous community engagement.International frameworks such as the Dakar Framework for Action, the Millennium Development Goals, and the Sustainable Development Goals have provided valuable direction in addressing marginalization. These initiatives emphasize inclusive education, gender equality, poverty reduction, and access to justice. They also encourage countries to develop context-specific strategies for marginalized populations.

India's National Education Policy (NEP) 2020 reflects the values enshrined in these international frameworks. It prioritizes inclusive and equitable education, with special emphasis on Socio-Economically Disadvantaged Groups (SEDGs). Through targeted measures like Special Education Zones, gender inclusion funds, and curriculum reform, NEP 2020 aims to bridge the gaps faced by marginalized learners.Moving forward, building an inclusive society requires collective effort. Government agencies, civil society, educators, and citizens must work together to dismantle systemic barriers and promote equity. Marginalization cannot be effectively addressed without acknowledging the inherent dignity and potential of every individual. Only by ensuring that all voices are heard and valued can we achieve true social justice and sustainable development.

KEY POINTS

- **Definition and Meaning of Marginalization:** Marginalization refers to the process by which certain individuals or groups are systematically excluded from meaningful participation in social, economic, political, and cultural life. This exclusion denies them access to resources, rights, and opportunities that are fundamental to social integration and development. Marginalization can be caused by a range of factors such as poverty, caste, ethnicity, gender, disability, or geographical location.
- **Characteristics of Marginalized Groups:** Marginalized groups often include Scheduled Castes (SCs), Scheduled Tribes (STs), educationally backward communities, and minorities defined by linguistic, regional, cultural, or religious differences. Women, children from rural and slum areas, and persons with special needs are also frequently marginalized. Common characteristics among these groups include limited access to quality education and healthcare, social stigma, political underrepresentation, and economic disadvantage. These groups often face structural barriers that hinder their full participation in society.

- **Indicators Used for Identifying Marginalized Groups:** Key indicators used to identify marginalized groups include poverty, which limits access to basic needs; relative isolation due to geographical or cultural separation; deprivation in terms of denial of rights and services; and exploitation through unfair labour and treatment. Discrimination based on caste, gender, or ability is a core indicator, alongside educational backwardness and general inequality in access to opportunities. The practice of untouchability, though legally abolished, persists in subtle forms and has deep historical and social roots in caste-based hierarchies.
- **International Perspectives and Policy Frameworks:** Globally, the Dakar Framework for Action (2000) emphasized inclusive and quality education for all, focusing on eliminating gender disparities and improving learning outcomes. The Millennium Development Goals (MDGs) sought to reduce poverty, improve education, and promote gender equality by 2015. Building on this, the Sustainable Development Goals (SDGs) adopted in 2015 aim to end all forms of inequality by 2030, with specific goals related to education (SDG 4), gender equality (SDG 5), and reduced inequalities (SDG 10). In India, the National Education Policy (NEP) 2020 echoes these global visions by prioritizing equity and inclusion through targeted measures like Special Education Zones, the Gender Inclusion Fund, and curriculum reforms to support Socio-Economically Disadvantaged Groups (SEDGs).

REFERENCES

1. Agarwal, S., & Taneja, S. (2005). All Slums are not Equal: Child Health Conditions among the Urban Poor. *Indian Paediatrics*, 42(3), 233-244. https://indianpediatrics.net/
2. Basu, A.R. (2010). *Tribal Development in India: A Study in Human Development*. Rawat Publications.
3. Baviskar, A. (2005). *In the Belly of the River: Tribal Conflicts over Development in the Narmada Valley* (2nd ed.). Oxford University Press.
4. Bhasin, K. (2000). *Understanding Gender*. Kali for Women.
5. Bhat, S. (2014). Rural Education in India: A Comprehensive Study of Challenges and Opportunities. *Indian Journal of Education*, 39(1), 49-63.
6. Bhatia, K., & Bhabha, J. (2007). India's Mid-day Meal Scheme: A Case Study in Incremental Reform. *Harvard School of Public Health*. https://www.hsph.harvard.edu
7. Bhattacharya, B. (2016). Life in Indian Slums: Study on Health, Education and Child Protection. *Social Change Review*, 14(2), 185-202. https://doi.org/10.1515/scr-2016-0012

8. Bose, A. (2001). *Urbanization in India: Challenges for the 21st Century*. Indian Council for Research on International Economic Relations.
9. Chandhoke, N. (2009). Pluralism, Secularism and the State in India. *Economic and Political Weekly*, 44(50), 35-43. https://www.epw.in
10. Chandrasekhar, C.P. (2013). Rural Education and Development in India. *Journal of Development Studies*, 49(1), 63-77. https://doi.org/10.1080/00220388.2013.790028
11. Desai, S., & Shyam, S. (2013). The Educational Divide in India: Bridging the Gap in Disadvantaged Groups. *Indian Journal of Social Development*, 13(4), 227-246. https://www.ijsd.org
12. Deshpande, A. (2011). *The Grammar of Caste: Economic Discrimination in Contemporary India*. Oxford University Press.
13. Government of India. (2006). *Social, Economic and Educational Status of the Muslim Community of India: A Report* (Sachar Committee Report).
14. Government of India. (2009). *Report of the National Commission for Religious and Linguistic Minorities*. Ministry of Minority Affairs. https://minorityaffairs.gov.in/
15. Government of India. (2015). *Rural Education Policy in India: An Assessment and Recommendations*. Ministry of Education. https://www.education.gov.in
16. Government of India. (2016). *The Rights of Persons with Disabilities Act, 2016*. Ministry of Social Justice and Empowerment. https://disabilityaffairs.gov.in/
17. Government of India. (2018). *Right to Education: A Critical Review of the National Policy on Education*. Ministry of Human Resource Development. https://www.mhrd.gov.in
18. Government of India. (2020). *National Policy on Education 2020*. Ministry of Education. https://www.education.gov.in
19. Government of India. (2021). *Annual Report 2020-21*. Ministry of Social Justice and Empowerment. https://socialjustice.gov.in/
20. Government of India. (2021). *Report of the Ministry of Women and Child Development*. https://wcd.nic.in/
21. Human Rights Watch. (2001). *Caste Discrimination: A Global Concern*. https://www.hrw.org/reports/2001/globalcaste/
22. Indian Institute of Dalit Studies. (2010). *Dalits in India: Search for a Common Destiny*. SAGE Publications.
23. Kothari, D. (2016). The Status of Educationally Backward Groups in India: Issues and Solutions. *Economic and Political Weekly*, 51(17), 67-75. https://www.epw.in
24. Kumar, K. (2012). The Impact of Socio-economic Status on Education Outcomes: Challenges and Opportunities. *Indian Journal of Education Research*, 8(2), 123-130. https://doi.org/10.1111/ijed.2012.8.2
25. Last, J.M. (Ed.). (2001). *A Dictionary of Public Health*. Oxford University Press.
26. Mahapatra, L.K. (2014). Cultural Rights of Minorities and Indigenous Peoples: Indian Experience. *Indian Anthropologist*, 44(1), 43-56.

27. Ministry of Education, Government of India. (2020). *National Education Policy 2020*. https://www.education.gov.in/sites/upload_files/mhrd/files/NEP_Final_English_0.pdf
28. Ministry of Housing and Urban Affairs, Government of India. (2020). *India Urban Report 2020*. https://mohua.gov.in/
29. Ministry of Human Resource Development, Government of India. (2015). *Report of the Committee for Evolving the New Education Policy*. https://www.education.gov.in
30. Ministry of Tribal Affairs, Government of India. (2021). *Annual Report 2020-21*. https://tribal.nic.in
31. Mitra, S. (2018). *Disability, Health and Human Development*. Palgrave Macmillan.
32. Nambissan, G.B. (2009). Exclusion and Discrimination in Schools: Experiences of Dalit Children. *IDS Bulletin*, 40(1), 55-63. https://doi.org/10.1111/j.1759-5436.2009.00009.x
33. Nambissan, G.B., & Suresh, S. (2012). *Inclusive Education and Marginalized Communities: Case Studies and Policy Implications*. SAGE Publications.
34. Narula, S. (2006). Equal by Law, Unequal by Caste: The "Untouchable" Condition in Critical Race Perspective. *Wisconsin International Law Journal*, 26(2), 255-304.
35. National Campaign on Dalit Human Rights. (2014). *Report on Caste-based Discrimination in India*. http://www.ncdhr.org.in/
36. National Commission for Scheduled Tribes. (2018). *Report on the Status of Scheduled Tribes in India*. https://ncst.nic.in
37. National Crime Records Bureau. (2022). *Crime in India Report*. Ministry of Home Affairs. https://ncrb.gov.in/
38. Nussbaum, M.C. (2000). *Women and Human Development: The Capabilities Approach*. Cambridge University Press.
39. Nussbaum, M.C. (2011). *Creating Capabilities: The Human Development Approach*. Harvard University Press.
40. Oliver, M. (1996). *Understanding Disability: From Theory to Practice*. Macmillan Education UK.
41. Planning Commission of India. (2008). *Development Challenges in Extremist Affected Areas: Report of an Expert Group*. https://niti.gov.in/planningcommission.gov.in
42. Ramachandran, V. (2004). Education and Inequality in India: Issues of Social Exclusion and Policy Implications. *Economic and Political Weekly*, 39(39), 4313-4320. https://www.epw.in
43. Ramachandran, V., & Sangeeta, G. (2005). *Education and Social Inequality: Understanding the Experiences of Disadvantaged Groups*. National Institute of Educational Planning and Administration. https://www.niepa.ac.in
44. Rawal, N. (2008). Social Inclusion and Exclusion: A Review. *Dhaulagiri Journal of Sociology and Anthropology*, 2, 161-180. https://doi.org/10.3126/dsaj.v2i0.1362

45. Sahu, P. (2015). Rural Poverty and Child Education in India: A Socio-economic Analysis. *Journal of Rural Studies*, 38, 203-212. https://doi.org/10.1016/j.jrurstud.2015.02.001
46. Save the Children. (2015). *Forgotten Voices: The World of Urban Children in India*. https://www.savethechildren.in/
47. Sen, A. (1999). *Development as Freedom*. Oxford University Press.
48. Sen, A. (2000). *Social Exclusion: Concept, Application, and Scrutiny*. Asian Development Bank. https://www.adb.org
49. Sen, A. (2006). *Identity and Violence: The Illusion of Destiny*. W.W. Norton & Company.

2 CHAPTER

Perspectives and Policies on Marginalization

INTRODUCTION

Marginalization refers to the systematic exclusion of certain individuals or groups from full participation in social, economic, political, and cultural life. It is often rooted in deep structural inequalities and perpetuated through entrenched ideologies and practices. Across time and regions, both Western and Eastern perspectives have offered various interpretations and responses to marginalization. These views, shaped by philosophical, political, and socio-cultural factors, provide unique insights into the causes and consequences of exclusion, as well as potential paths toward inclusion and justice.

In the Western tradition, Karl Marx laid a foundational framework for understanding marginalization through his critique of capitalism. According to Marx, economic structures create class divisions, leading to the oppression of the proletariat by the bourgeoisie. Marginalization, in this context, is a byproduct of capitalist exploitation, where labourers are alienated from the products of their work and from meaningful participation in society. Paulo Freire, a Brazilian educator and philosopher, built upon this framework by emphasizing the role of education in liberation. His pedagogy of the oppressed advocates for a participatory and dialogic form of education that empowers marginalized communities to question and transform the social conditions of their oppression. Eastern perspectives on marginalization present different but complementary insights. Mahatma Gandhi envisioned a just society based on non-violence, self-reliance, and the upliftment of the most oppressed, whom he referred to as "Harijans" or "children of God." His approach to marginalization emphasized moral responsibility, simplicity, and village self-governance. Dr. B.R. Ambedkar, in contrast, advocated for a more radical transformation of the caste system through legal and political reform. As a social reformer and architect of the Indian Constitution, Ambedkar championed the rights of Dalits and other oppressed communities, promoting affirmative action and legal safeguards. Swami Vivekananda also contributed significantly to the discourse on social inclusion, advocating for the upliftment of the poor and marginalized through education, spiritual development, and social service.

Marginalized groups possess inherent rights that must be recognized and protected to ensure justice and equality. These include the right to exist with dignity, freedom from discrimination, and protection of their cultural, religious, linguistic, and social identities.

Moreover, their right to participate in public life and decision-making processes is fundamental to any democratic society. Ensuring educational access and fostering cultural expression are equally important in affirming their identity and enabling them to contribute meaningfully to national development. India's policy framework has attempted to address marginalization through various constitutional and legal provisions. Scheduled Castes and Scheduled Tribes have been accorded special protections and entitlements, including reservations in education, employment, and political representation. However, these measures have seen mixed results in practice. While they have enabled access to opportunities for some, systemic barriers and social prejudices continue to hinder the full realization of rights for many within these communities.

Forest, land, and revenue policies have historically played a significant role in the marginalization of tribal communities. The colonial and post-colonial state often prioritized resource extraction and economic development over the rights and livelihoods of indigenous populations. Displacement due to development projects such as dams, mining, and infrastructure has exacerbated the vulnerability of tribal communities, leading to loss of land, culture, and autonomy. In this context, land alienation and restricted access to traditional resources have had far-reaching consequences on their social and economic wellbeing. The impact of development on tribal communities is particularly evident in states like Kerala. While Kerala is often hailed for its progressive social indicators, tribal populations in the state have continued to experience neglect and underdevelopment. Issues such as landlessness, lack of access to quality education and healthcare, and cultural assimilation pressures remain persistent. Government initiatives and civil society efforts have attempted to address these gaps, but structural inequalities and policy implementation failures have limited their impact.

Panchayati Raj Institutions (PRIs) have emerged as a crucial mechanism for grassroots democracy and inclusive development. In theory, PRIs provide

Scheduled Castes and Scheduled Tribes with a platform to participate in decision-making processes at the local level. Constitutional amendments mandating reservations in local bodies have empowered many marginalized individuals to hold leadership positions. However, challenges such as tokenism, lack of capacity building, and interference from dominant groups often undermine the effectiveness of these institutions in truly representing and addressing the concerns of marginalized communities.The role of community-based organizations, NGOs, and civil society in supporting the rights of marginalized groups is increasingly recognized as essential. These actors help bridge the gap between policy and practice, advocate for rights, and provide critical services in education, healthcare, and legal aid. Their efforts have brought attention to the lived experiences of marginalized people and pressured governments to be more accountable and inclusive in their governance frameworks.

In conclusion, addressing marginalization requires a multifaceted and inclusive approach that draws on diverse ideological perspectives and is grounded in rights-based policy frameworks. It entails not only legal reforms and affirmative action but also a shift in societal attitudes, participatory governance, and equitable development. As India continues to grapple with the challenges of inclusion, the insights of thinkers like Marx, Freire, Gandhi, Ambedkar, and Vivekananda remain deeply relevant in envisioning a just and equal society for all.

WESTERN AND EASTERN PERSPECTIVES ON MARGINALIZATION: A COMPARATIVE IDEOLOGICAL REFLECTION

Marginalization, the process by which certain groups are pushed to the edge of society, is a universal phenomenon. Western and Eastern thinkers have addressed this issue from distinct philosophical and cultural vantage points. Karl Marx, the prominent Western theorist, viewed marginalization primarily through the lens of class struggle. He argued that the capitalist system inherently exploits the proletariat, leading to alienation and social exclusion. For Marx, the solution lay in the overthrow of the bourgeoisie and the establishment of a classless, socialist society where the means of production are owned collectively.

In a similar yet contextually unique direction, Paulo Freire, a Brazilian educator and philosopher, emphasized the role of education in addressing marginalization. His concept of "conscientization" highlighted the need for the oppressed to develop a critical awareness of their reality through dialogue and reflection. Freire viewed traditional education systems as oppressive and advocated for a pedagogy that empowers marginalized communities to become active participants in their liberation. His ideas resonate deeply with movements that seek to transform oppressive social structures through participatory and inclusive education.

Eastern thinkers have responded to marginalization within the specific sociopolitical realities of colonialism, caste, and cultural oppression. Mahatma Gandhi emphasized non-violent resistance and the upliftment of marginalized communities, particularly the "Harijans" or the so-called untouchables. He promoted the idea of Sarvodaya (welfare of all) and envisioned a society rooted in truth, equality, and spiritual harmony. However, Gandhi's approach was critiqued by Dr. B.R. Ambedkar, who saw caste as a deeply entrenched system of social exclusion that could not be reformed merely through moral appeals. Ambedkar, a staunch advocate for the rights of Dalits, argued for legal and institutional reforms to eradicate caste-based discrimination. His emphasis on education, constitutional rights, and social justice positioned him as a radical voice for the truly marginalized in India.

Swami Vivekananda, though rooted in the spiritual traditions of the East, also addressed marginalization through the lens of social upliftment. He believed that the regeneration of India lay in the empowerment of the poor and the downtrodden through education, character-building, and the revival of spiritual values. He emphasized that true religion lies in serving humanity, thus integrating spiritual thought with social action. Together, these thinkers from both Western and Eastern traditions offer diverse yet converging perspectives on marginalization, advocating for structural change, education, and moral awakening as pathways to an inclusive and equitable society.

KARL MARX'S PERSPECTIVE ON MARGINALIZATION

Karl Marx, one of the most influential Western thinkers, analysed marginalization through the lens of class struggle and economic inequality. In his critique of capitalism, Marx argued that society is divided into two major classes: the bourgeoisie, who control the means of production, and the proletariat, who must sell their labour to survive. This capitalist structure, he claimed, inherently marginalizes the working class by exploiting their labour for profit while concentrating wealth and power in the hands of a few. Marx introduced the concept of alienation, explaining that workers become estranged from the products they create, the process of labour, their fellow workers, and ultimately themselves. This alienation is not merely a psychological state but a material condition rooted in the exploitative relationship between labour and capital. As the capitalist mode of production advances, the working class becomes increasingly dehumanized, reduced to mere tools in the pursuit of profit.

Marx believed that this form of marginalization was not a natural or permanent condition but a result of historically specific economic arrangements. He emphasized that the only way to eliminate marginalization was through revolutionary praxis, where the proletariat would rise up, seize control of the means of production, and establish a classless, socialist society. This transformation, according to Marx, would abolish private property, dismantle class hierarchies, and create conditions for true human freedom and equality. His ideas laid the foundation for critical theories of social justice and have inspired numerous liberation movements around the world. Marx's perspective on marginalization continues to be relevant today, as it highlights how economic systems and power relations contribute to the systemic exclusion of large segments of society.

Key Aspects of Marx's Perspective

- **Class Struggle:** Marx believed that history is shaped by the conflict between different social classes, primarily over control of the means of production. The bourgeoisie exploits the proletariat, leading to class conflict.
- **Alienation:** Marx identified four types of alienation:
  (a) *Alienation from the Product:* Workers have no control over what they produce.
  (b) *Alienation from the Process:* Repetitive tasks erode creativity and autonomy.
  (c) *Alienation from Others:* Workers view each other as competitors.
  (d) *Alienation from Self:* Work becomes a means to survival rather than a fulfilling activity.
- **Bureaucracy and Marginalization:** Marx argued that bureaucracy serves as a tool for the ruling class to maintain dominance, perpetuating inequality and marginalization. Bureaucratic systems prioritize private interests over public needs, further exploiting the working class.
- **Empowerment through Decentralization:** Marx's ideas suggest that decentralization and participatory governance can help address marginalization by involving local communities in decision-making processes and promoting transparency and accountability.

Overall, Marx's perspective on marginalization emphasizes the need to address the root causes of exploitation and inequality in capitalist systems, promoting a more equitable society through the empowerment of the working class.

PAULO FREIRE'S PERSPECTIVE ON MARGINALIZATION

Paulo Freire, a prominent Brazilian educator and philosopher, offered a transformative approach to understanding and addressing marginalization, particularly through education. In his influential work *Pedagogy of the Oppressed,* Freire argued that traditional education systems often serve to maintain the status quo by treating students as passive recipients of knowledge—a method he called the "banking model" of education. In this system, the marginalized are taught to accept their oppression rather than question or challenge it. Freire believed that education should instead be dialogical and participatory, enabling the oppressed to become aware of their social reality through a process he called *conscientização*, or critical consciousness. This awareness empowers individuals to recognize the injustices they face and to take action to transform their conditions. For Freire, marginalization is not only about economic deprivation but also about the denial of voice, agency, and participation in shaping one's own destiny.

Freire's ideology promotes the idea that liberation from marginalization begins with education that respects the knowledge, experiences, and cultures of the oppressed. He emphasized that true learning occurs when educators and learners engage in mutual dialogue, questioning the world together and co-creating knowledge. This process encourages the marginalized to see themselves not as passive victims but as active agents of change. Freire's vision extended beyond the classroom, advocating for a more just and equitable society in which all individuals have the opportunity to participate meaningfully. His ideas have had a profound influence on liberation movements, critical pedagogy, and educational reforms worldwide. By linking education with social justice, Freire provided a powerful framework for addressing the root causes of marginalization and for empowering communities to transform their realities.

Key Aspects of Freire's Perspective

- **Pedagogy of the Oppressed:** Freire's work emphasizes the need for critical consciousness and collective action to challenge oppressive systems and promote social change.
- **Conscientization:** Freire believed that marginalized individuals must become aware of their own oppression and take an active role in transforming their reality.
- **Empowerment through Education:** Freire advocated for education as a means of empowerment, promoting critical thinking, and challenging dominant ideologies.
- **Dialogue and Collaboration:** Freire emphasized the importance of dialogue and collaboration between the oppressed and the oppressors, highlighting the need for mutual understanding and respect.

Freire's Ideas on Marginalization

- **Cultural Silence:** Freire argued that marginalized groups are often silenced and excluded from dominant cultural narratives, perpetuating their marginalization.

- **Power Dynamics:** Freire highlighted the power imbalance between the dominant and marginalized groups, emphasizing the need for critical analysis and collective action to challenge these dynamics.
- **Liberation through Praxis:** Freire believed that marginalized groups must engage in praxis, combining reflection and action, to challenge oppressive systems and achieve liberation.

Implications of Freire's Perspective

- **Critical Pedagogy:** Freire's work has influenced critical pedagogy, emphasizing the need for education to be a transformative and empowering experience for marginalized groups.
- **Social Justice:** Freire's ideas have been applied to social justice movements, highlighting the importance of collective action and critical consciousness in challenging oppressive systems.

Overall, Freire's perspective on marginalization emphasizes the need for critical consciousness, collective action, and empowerment through education to challenge oppressive systems and promote social change.

MAHATMA GANDHI'S PERSPECTIVE ON MARGINALIZATION

Mahatma Gandhi, one of the most influential Eastern thinkers and leaders of the Indian independence movement, approached marginalization through a deeply ethical and spiritual framework. Gandhi believed that the root of social exclusion lay not only in political or economic systems but also in moral decay and the loss of human values such as compassion, truth, and nonviolence. His concept of Sarvodaya the welfare of allreflected his commitment to uplifting the most disadvantaged members of society, particularly the Dalits, whom he referred to as Harijans (children of God). Gandhi opposed untouchability and campaigned for the integration of Dalits into mainstream society, advocating for their access to education, sanitation, and equal rights. However, his approach was more reformist than revolutionary; he sought to change the hearts and minds of individuals through moral persuasion and nonviolent resistance, rather than through systemic overhaul.

Gandhi's philosophy emphasized Swaraj (self-rule), not just as political independence from colonial rule but as individual and community self-governance rooted in ethical living and service to others. He believed that true freedom could only be achieved when the most marginalized were empowered to live with dignity and equality. Gandhi encouraged a return to village-based economies, simple living, and manual labour, which he saw as antidotes to the alienation and exploitation caused by industrial capitalism and colonialism. Although his efforts were sometimes criticized particularly by thinkers like B.R. Ambedkar, who felt Gandhi's methods did not adequately address structural caste inequalities Gandhi's ideology played a crucial role in raising awareness about the plight of marginalized groups in India. His legacy continues to inspire nonviolent movements for justice, equality, and human dignity across the world.

Key Aspects of Gandhi's Perspective

- **Sarvodaya:** Gandhi's concept of Sarvodaya, or the welfare of all, emphasizes the need for equitable distribution of resources and opportunities.
- **Harijan Upliftment:** Gandhi worked tirelessly for the eradication of untouchability and the upliftment of the oppressed castes, whom he referred to as Harijans (children of God).
- **Economic Empowerment:** Gandhi believed in the importance of economic self-sufficiency and advocated for rural development, cottage industries, and cooperative movements to empower marginalized communities.
- **Non-Violent Resistance:** Gandhi's philosophy of non-violent resistance, or Satyagraha, emphasizes the power of non-cooperation and civil disobedience in challenging unjust systems and promoting social change.

Gandhi's Ideas on Marginalization

- **Critique of Caste System:** Gandhi criticized the caste system for perpetuating social inequality and advocated for its reform.
- **Empowerment of Women:** Gandhi believed in the importance of women's empowerment and their role in social change, encouraging them to participate in the freedom struggle and community development.
- **Inclusive Development:** Gandhi's vision of development emphasizes the need for inclusivity, sustainability, and social justice, ensuring that the benefits of development reach all sections of society.

Implications of Gandhi's Perspective

- **Social Justice Movements:** Gandhi's ideas have influenced social justice movements in India and globally, emphasizing the importance of non-violent resistance and collective action in challenging oppressive systems.
- **Community Development:** Gandhi's emphasis on rural development, self-sufficiency, and community participation has inspired community development initiatives and programs aimed at empowering marginalized communities.

Overall, Gandhi's perspective on marginalization highlights the importance of social justice, equality, and non-violent resistance in promoting the welfare of all and challenging oppressive systems.

DR. B.R. AMBEDKAR'S PERSPECTIVE ON MARGINALIZATION

Dr. B.R. Ambedkar, a prominent Indian jurist, economist, and social reformer, offered one of the most powerful and uncompromising critiques of marginalization in the context of caste oppression in India. As a Dalit himself, Ambedkar experienced firsthand the severe discrimination and exclusion faced by those at the bottom of the caste hierarchy. Unlike reformist thinkers who sought to change attitudes within the existing caste system, Ambedkar rejected the caste system entirely, viewing it as inherently unequal and oppressive. He argued that caste-based marginalization was not merely a social or cultural issue, but a systemic form of inequality enshrined in religion, law, and tradition. In his seminal work Annihilation of Caste, Ambedkar called for the total eradication of caste, asserting that social justice could only be achieved through radical structural reform and the assertion of equal rights for all, regardless of birth.

Ambedkar believed that true liberation for the marginalized could only be secured through education, political representation, and legal empowerment. He championed the rights of Dalits and other oppressed communities by playing a pivotal role in drafting the Indian Constitution, embedding principles of equality, non-discrimination, and affirmative action into the legal fabric of the nation. For Ambedkar, democracy was not just a political system but a means to ensure social justice and human dignity for the marginalized. He emphasized that mere symbolic inclusion was not enough; real change required dismantling the deeply rooted social hierarchies that perpetuated exclusion. His ideology continues to resonate in contemporary struggles against caste, class, and social injustice, both in India and globally, offering a transformative vision of equality and human rights for the oppressed.

Key Aspects of Ambedkar's Perspective

- **Caste System Critique:** Ambedkar vehemently criticized the caste system, considering it a major obstacle to social equality. He advocated for its annihilation, believing that it perpetuated discrimination and oppression against Dalits and women.
- **Social Justice:** Ambedkar's concept of social justice emphasized equal rights and opportunities for all, regardless of caste or gender. He believed in education as a powerful tool for socio-economic empowerment and advocated for fair labour rights.

- **Women's Rights:** Ambedkar championed women's rights and emancipation, introducing the Hindu Code Bill to provide equal rights in inheritance, marriage, and the workforce. He saw gender equality as essential to a just society.
- **Constitutional Reform:** As the principal architect of the Indian Constitution, Ambedkar ensured the inclusion of provisions for protecting civil liberties and promoting social justice. He introduced the Reservation system to correct historical injustices.
- **Buddhism and Social Reform:** Ambedkar's conversion to Buddhism was a significant move towards social reform. He reinterpreted Buddhism to align with modern, socially emancipatory aspirations, paving the way for its revival as a force for social reform and empowerment.

Impact of Ambedkar's Perspective

- **Inspiring Social Movements:** Ambedkar's ideas and ideals continue to inspire social and political movements in India, advocating for equality and justice.
- **Global Relevance:** His thoughts resonate with international social justice movements, emphasizing the universality of his message.
- **Legacy:** Ambedkar's legacy as a social reformer, jurist, economist, and politician remains a beacon of hope for marginalized communities, guiding the pursuit of equality and justice in modern times.

SWAMI VIVEKANANDA'S PERSPECTIVE ON MARGINALIZATION

Swami Vivekananda, a key figure in the Eastern philosophical and spiritual tradition, addressed marginalization through the lens of spiritual humanism and social reform. Deeply influenced by Vedantic philosophy, he believed in the inherent divinity and equality of all human beings, regardless of caste, class, religion, or gender. Vivekananda saw the neglect of the poor and downtrodden as a profound moral failure, not just a social issue. He emphasized that true religion lies in serving humanity, famously stating, "They alone live who live for others." He criticized the rigid caste system and religious orthodoxy that perpetuated inequality and exclusion in Indian society. For Vivekananda, education was the primary tool for empowerment; he advocated for an inclusive and holistic form of education that would build character, instil self-confidence, and awaken the inner strength of the marginalized.

Vivekananda's vision of social upliftment was deeply rooted in action and service. Through the establishment of the Ramakrishna Mission, he promoted a practical form of spirituality that addressed real-world problems such as poverty, illiteracy, and social discrimination. Unlike purely political or economic approaches, Vivekananda's philosophy emphasized the unity of material progress and spiritual growth. He believed that the regeneration of India would be possible only when the oppressed masses were spiritually awakened and given equal opportunities to grow. His teachings continue to inspire social and educational initiatives across India and beyond, advocating for a society where dignity, compassion, and justice are extended to all. Vivekananda's ideology thus offers a unique blend of spiritual wisdom and social commitment, presenting an Eastern approach to marginalization rooted in universal human values.

- **Women's Empowerment:** Vivekananda advocated for women's rights and equality, believing that women's liberation is crucial for societal progress. He worked tirelessly to promote women's education and empowerment, and his ideas have inspired many to work towards this goal.
- **Criticizing Social Inequality:** Vivekananda criticized the social and economic inequalities prevalent in Indian society, emphasizing the need for collective action to address these issues. He believed that education and self-empowerment are essential for overcoming marginalization.
- **Vedanta and Spiritual Awakening:** Vivekananda's teachings emphasize the importance of spiritual growth and self-realization. He believed that every individual has the potential for spiritual awakening, regardless of their social background or circumstances.
- **Addressing Marginalization:** According to Vivekananda, addressing marginalization requires a multifaceted approach that includes education, economic empowerment, and social reform. He believed that by working together, individuals and communities can create a more just and equitable society.
- Vivekananda's ideas have had a lasting impact on Indian society and continue to inspire social and philosophical movements today. His emphasis on women's empowerment, education, and spiritual growth has made him a revered figure in Indian history.

RENAISSANCE IN KERALA: INFLUENCE OF SREE NARAYANA GURU AND AYYANKALI

The Kerala Renaissance was a powerful socio-cultural reform movement that emerged in the 19th and early 20th centuries, challenging deep-rooted caste hierarchies, superstitions, and social inequalities. It was marked by the rise of reformers who sought to create a more equitable and progressive society. Two of the most significant figures in this movement were Sree Narayana Guru and Ayyankali, both of whom emerged from marginalized communities and played crucial roles in shaping modern Kerala's values of social justice, equality, and human dignity.Sree Narayana Guru, a spiritual leader and philosopher, focused on eradicating caste discrimination through peaceful means and moral reform. Born into the Ezhava community, which was socially ostracized, Guru challenged the dominance of Brahmanical rituals and caste-based exclusion. His famous declaration, "One caste, one religion, one God for mankind," became a rallying cry for social unity. He established temples open to all castes and emphasized the importance of education and spiritual awakening. By founding the Sree Narayana Dharma Paripalana (SNDP) Yogam, he organized collective efforts to uplift oppressed communities. His approach combined spiritual enlightenment with social activism, making him a central figure in Kerala's renaissance.

Ayyankali, on the other hand, took a more confrontational and political approach to fight caste oppression. A leader from the Pulayar community, he strongly opposed the inhumane practices of untouchability and the denial of basic rights to Dalits. Ayyankali focused on gaining access to education and public spaces for the oppressed. He started schools for Dalit children and led movements to assert the right to walk on public roads - an act that faced violent resistance from upper-caste groups. His formation of the Sadhu Jana Paripalana Sangham in 1907 was a significant step in organizing Dalits for collective empowerment. Through protests, negotiations, and grassroots activism, Ayyankali played a foundational role in democratizing public life in Kerala.

Together, Sree Narayana Guru and Ayyankali laid the foundation for a just and inclusive society in Kerala. While Guru used spiritual and philosophical tools to promote equality, Ayyankali relied on direct action and political mobilization. Their complementary approaches addressed both the internalized and institutional aspects of caste-based marginalization. The Kerala Renaissance, shaped by their efforts, not only reformed social structures but also influenced future political and educational developments in the state. Their legacy lives on in Kerala's continued commitment to social justice, secularism, and democratic values.

Sree Narayana Guru's Contributions

- **Philosophy:** Guru's philosophy centred around "One Caste, One Religion, One God for All," emphasizing the importance of equality and unity among people.
- **Temple Consecration:** He consecrated 43 temples across South India, challenging the traditional Brahminical dominance in temple rituals. Notably, he installed a Sivalinga at Aruvippuram in 1888, sparking the "Aruvippuram Revolution".
- **Social Reform:** Guru worked tirelessly to eradicate untouchability and social inequality, promoting education and self-empowerment among the backward classes.

- **Literary Contributions:** He wrote 45 books in Malayalam, Sanskrit, and Tamil, including "AathmopadeshShathakam" and "Dharsanamala".
- **Organizations:** Guru founded the Sree Narayana Dharma Paripalana Yogam (SNDP) in 1903, which became a pivotal organization in promoting social reform and empowerment.

Ayyankali's Contributions

- **Social Equality:** Ayyankali fought for the rights of the marginalized and oppressed, advocating for social equality and justice.
- **Education:** He emphasized the importance of education in empowering the backward classes and promoting social mobility.
- **Interaction with Sree Narayana Guru:** Ayyankali met Sree Narayana Guru in 1912 at Balaramapuram, highlighting the convergence of their reformist ideals.

Impact of the Kerala Renaissance

The Kerala Renaissance, led by Sree Narayana Guru and Ayyankali, had a profound impact on the region's social and cultural landscape. Their efforts paved the way for:

- **Social Reform:** Challenging traditional hierarchies and promoting social equality.
- **Education:** Emphasizing the importance of education in empowering marginalized communities.
- **Cultural Revival:** Revitalizing Kerala's cultural heritage and promoting artistic expression.
- Their legacy continues to inspire social and cultural movements in Kerala, shaping the region's identity and promoting a more equitable society.

FACTORS BEHIND THE EMERGENCE OF MARGINALIZATION

Marginalization refers to the process through which certain individuals or groups are pushed to the edges of society, deprived of opportunities, resources, and recognition. One of the most fundamental factors behind marginalization is the lack of equality. Social and economic inequalities result in uneven access to education, healthcare, employment, and participation in public life. When societies are structured in a way that benefits a few while excluding others, it creates deep divisions that marginalize vulnerable populations. Economic inequality, in particular, reinforces a cycle of poverty, where marginalized groups remain deprived across generations. Without equal access to resources and decision-making, marginalized communities are unable to uplift themselves, further deepening their exclusion.

Power dynamics also play a critical role in the emergence of marginalization. In most societies, certain groups control political, economic, and social power, while others are systematically denied influence. This concentration of power enables dominant groups to set rules, values, and policies that favour their interests. Marginalized groups, lacking both formal and informal power, are unable to assert their needs or participate meaningfully in governance. This imbalance perpetuates exclusion, as powerful groups often resist changes that could empower the marginalized. Institutions such as the legal system, education, and media often reflect and reinforce these power structures, limiting the opportunities for marginalized voices to be heard or acknowledged.

Ethnicity and caste are deeply rooted social structures that significantly contribute to marginalization. In multi-ethnic societies, dominant ethnic groups often marginalize minorities by denying them cultural recognition, political representation, and economic opportunities. Discrimination based on ethnic identity leads to social exclusion and the denial of basic rights. Similarly, caste-based marginalization, especially in countries like India, enforces a rigid social hierarchy where individuals from lower castes, particularly Dalits and tribal communities, are historically denied dignity, education, and social mobility. These forms of discrimination are institutionalized and perpetuated through social norms and practices, making it difficult for affected groups to break free from marginalization.

Geographical factors also significantly influence marginalization. Communities living in remote, rural, or underdeveloped regions often lack access to basic services such as clean water, healthcare, education, and transportation. Urban-centric development policies tend to ignore these regions, creating a stark urban-rural divide. People in geographically isolated areas may also be excluded from political processes, information networks, and economic opportunities. Furthermore, displacement due to natural disasters, armed conflict, or infrastructure projects can lead to forced marginalization, pushing people into unfamiliar environments where they lack support systems. Thus, geography intersects with social, political, and economic factors to create multiple layers of exclusion, making the fight against marginalization a complex and ongoing challenge. Marginalization can emerge from various interconnected factors, including:

- **Inequality:** Economic, social, and cultural disparities can lead to marginalization, where certain groups are denied access to resources, opportunities, and rights.
- **Power Dynamics:** Imbalances in power can result in dominant groups exploiting or oppressing marginalized groups, perpetuating inequality and exclusion.

- **Ethnicity:** Ethnic differences can lead to marginalization, particularly when certain groups are excluded from decision-making processes or face discrimination based on their identity.
- **Caste:** Caste-based systems can perpetuate marginalization, where certain groups are considered inferior or impure, leading to social exclusion and limited opportunities.
- **Geographical Area:** Geographical location can contribute to marginalization, particularly in rural or remote areas where access to resources, services, and opportunities may be limited.

Interconnectedness of Factors

These factors can intersect and compound, leading to complex forms of marginalization. For instance:

(a) *Intersectionality:* The intersection of multiple factors, such as caste, ethnicity, and geographical location, can exacerbate marginalization.

(b) *Cumulative Disadvantage:* The accumulation of disadvantages over time can further entrench marginalization.

Consequences of Marginalization

Marginalization can have severe consequences, including:

(a) *Social Exclusion:* Marginalized groups may be excluded from social, economic, and political processes.

(b) *Limited Opportunities:* Marginalization can limit access to education, employment, and healthcare.

(c) *Poor Health Outcomes:* Marginalized groups may experience poorer health outcomes due to limited access to healthcare and other resources.

Addressing Marginalization

Addressing marginalization requires a comprehensive approach that includes:

(a) *Policy Interventions:* Policies aimed at promoting equality and inclusion can help address marginalization.

(b) *Social Movements:* Social movements can raise awareness and mobilize action to address marginalization.

(c) *Community Empowerment:* Empowering marginalized communities can help them access resources and opportunities. By understanding the complex factors behind marginalization, we can work towards creating a more inclusive and equitable society.

RIGHTS OF MARGINALIZED GROUPS

Marginalized groups, due to social, economic, cultural, or political exclusion, are often denied basic human rights. One of the most fundamental rights is the right to exist with dignity and security. This includes protection from violence, displacement, and systemic neglect. Marginalized communitiessuch as indigenous peoples, Dalits, persons with disabilities, ethnic and religious minoritieshave historically faced threats to their existence, whether through conflict, environmental degradation, or discriminatory policies. Recognizing their right to life and survival requires legal frameworks that ensure safety, access to basic necessities, and the ability to live without fear.

The right to non-discrimination is central to the protection of marginalized groups. Discrimination based on caste, gender, ethnicity, religion, disability, or language perpetuates cycles of exclusion and inequality. Legal provisions such as anti-discrimination laws, affirmative action, and equal opportunity policies are essential in creating a level playing field. International human rights instruments, such as the Universal Declaration of Human Rights and the International Convention on the Elimination of All Forms of Racial Discrimination, affirm the principle of equality before the law. Non-discrimination also means dismantling institutional barriers that restrict access to justice, employment, education, and healthcare for marginalized populations.

Protecting the cultural, religious, and linguistic identities of marginalized groups is crucial to preserving their dignity and heritage. These groups have the right to express their beliefs, speak their languages, and practice their traditions without fear of assimilation or erasure. In multicultural societies, respecting cultural diversity enriches national identity and promotes social harmony. Many constitutions and international treaties, such as the UN Declaration on the Rights of Indigenous Peoples, recognize the importance of safeguarding these identities. Protection of identity also includes ensuring land rights, intellectual property rights related to traditional knowledge, and media representation that reflects cultural diversity.

Finally, marginalized groups must have the right to participate in public life and decision-making processes. True democracy requires the inclusion of all voices, especially those historically silenced. This includes the right to vote, run for public office, join political parties, and be part of community organizations. Representation in local and national bodies ensures that policies are more inclusive and responsive to the needs of all citizens. Participation also extends to educational and economic development, where marginalized individuals must have opportunities to shape their futures. Upholding these rights is not only a moral obligation but a key to building equitable, just, and inclusive societies.

Right to Exist: A Fundamental Right of Marginalized Groups

The right to exist is the most basic and essential human right, yet it is one most often threatened for marginalized groups. For many such communities including indigenous peoples, Dalits, religious minorities, LGBTQ+ individuals, and people with disabilities this right has historically been violated through systemic violence, neglect, and denial of basic needs. The right to exist not only means freedom from physical harm or persecution, but also includes the right to live with dignity, to access food, shelter, healthcare, and security. Marginalized communities often face threats to their very survival due to poverty, displacement, environmental degradation, or targeted violence. Ensuring their right to exist means establishing strong legal protections, humanitarian safeguards, and social safety nets that affirm their place and value in society.

Furthermore, the right to exist involves recognition acknowledging the historical injustices and current vulnerabilities that put marginalized lives at risk. This includes addressing issues such as forced evictions of indigenous tribes, hate crimes against minorities, and gender-based violence against transgender people. Governments and international bodies must go beyond mere legal acknowledgment and take proactive steps to secure and protect the existence of these groups. This right is the foundation upon which all other rightssuch as education, equality, and participationcan be built. Without the guarantee of existence, marginalized voices cannot be heard, and justice remains an illusion. Therefore, the right to exist must be prioritized in all human rights frameworks and national policies.

Right to Non-Discrimination: Ensuring Equality for Marginalized Groups

The right to non-discrimination is a cornerstone of human rights and is essential for achieving justice and equality in any society. For marginalized groups including those discriminated against based on caste, ethnicity, religion, gender, disability, or sexual orientation this right ensures equal treatment under the law and equal access to opportunities. Discrimination often operates both overtly and subtly, in the form of unequal wages, limited access to quality education and healthcare, restricted political participation, and social exclusion. Legal frameworks such as constitutional guarantees, anti-discrimination laws, and affirmative action policies are crucial to dismantle these systemic barriers. International human rights instruments like the International Convention on the Elimination of all Forms of Racial Discrimination and the Convention on the Rights of Persons with Disabilities also underscore the global commitment to protecting this right.

However, legal protections alone are not enough; the right to non-discrimination must be actively enforced and socially embedded. Marginalized individuals must feel safe and empowered to seek justice when their rights are violated. This requires accessible legal aid, education on rights, and inclusive public policies. Social institutions such as schools, workplaces, and media must also promote diversity and challenge stereotypes that reinforce inequality. By fostering environments where diversity is respected and protected, societies move closer to real equality. Upholding the right to non-discrimination not only benefits marginalized communities but strengthens democratic values, social cohesion, and sustainable development for all.

Protection of Identity: A Fundamental Right of Marginalized Groups

The protection of identity is a critical component of human rights, especially for marginalized groups whose cultural, linguistic, religious, or social identities have historically been devalued or suppressed. Identity is closely linked to dignity, belonging, and community, and when it is denied or threatened, it leads to psychological, social, and cultural harm. For indigenous peoples, ethnic minorities, LGBTQ+ individuals, and linguistic communities, the right to maintain and express their identity is essential for survival and self-respect. International frameworks such as the UN Declaration on the Rights of Indigenous Peoples emphasize the right of communities to preserve their traditions, languages, customs, and spiritual practices without coercion or assimilation.

Protecting identity also means safeguarding against policies or societal pressures that aim to erase or dilute the distinctiveness of marginalized groups. This includes ensuring access to mother-tongue education, religious freedom, traditional attire, cultural ceremonies, and representation in media and political spaces. When identity is protected, marginalized individuals are empowered to participate fully in society without sacrificing who they are. Moreover, the celebration of diverse identities strengthens multiculturalism and social harmony. Governments and institutions have a duty to not only recognize but actively support and protect the unique identities of marginalized communities through inclusive laws, education, and public policy.

Right to Participate in Public Life and Decision Making

The right to participate in public life and decision-making is a cornerstone of democratic governance, and it is essential for the empowerment of marginalized groups. Historically, marginalized communities such as women, Dalits, indigenous peoples, and ethnic minorities—have been excluded from political processes and decision-making forums. This exclusion perpetuates their marginalization and limits their ability to advocate for their rights, voice their concerns, or influence policies that directly affect their lives. The right to political participation is not only a fundamental human right but also crucial for the creation of inclusive, fair, and just societies. By ensuring that marginalized groups have equal opportunities to vote, run for office, join political parties, and participate in policymaking, democracies can reflect the diverse needs and aspirations of all citizens.

Participation in public life also extends beyond formal political engagement. Marginalized groups must be included in community-level decision-making processes, public consultations, and the development of policies affecting their communities. This ensures that their unique experiences, needs, and concerns are addressed. In addition, representation in education, employment, and media is vital for fostering a sense of belonging and shaping public discourse. Social inclusion through active participation allows marginalized individuals to challenge stereotypes, advocate for justice, and shape their futures. Governments, therefore, have a responsibility to remove barriers that prevent marginalized groups from participating fully in public life and to create environments that promote equal engagement and representation.

Other Educational, Cultural, Religious, and Linguistic Rights of Marginalized Groups

In addition to fundamental human rights, marginalized groups have specific educational, cultural, religious, and linguistic rights that are critical to preserving their dignity and fostering equality. The right to education is particularly significant for marginalized communities, who often face systemic barriers in accessing quality schooling. Discriminatory practices, economic constraints, and social stigmas often result in lower literacy rates and limited educational opportunities for groups such as Dalits, indigenous peoples, and girls from rural or low-income families. Governments and international bodies must ensure that educational policies and practices are inclusive, accessible, and culturally sensitive, allowing marginalized children and adults the chance to fully participate in society and achieve social mobility. This includes providing scholarships, language-based educational programs, and removing institutional biases that hinder educational access.

Equally important is the protection of cultural, religious, and linguistic rights, which allow marginalized groups to maintain their unique identities and practices. For example, indigenous peoples and ethnic minorities have the right to practice their religion, celebrate their cultural traditions, and speak their native languages without fear of persecution or assimilation. Educational curricula should reflect the diverse cultural backgrounds of students and incorporate lessons that promote tolerance and understanding. The protection of cultural heritage, religious freedom, and linguistic diversity is vital for the social inclusion and self-determination of marginalized groups. Governments should enact laws and policies that preserve and promote these rights, ensuring that marginalized communities are not only protected from cultural erasure but also empowered to thrive in a pluralistic society.

POLICIES AND THEIR IMPACT ON MARGINALIZED COMMUNITIES: FOREST, LAND, AND REVENUE POLICIES

Forest, land, and revenue policies have historically played a significant role in shaping the lives of marginalized communities, particularly indigenous peoples, Dalits, and landless labourers. Forest policies introduced during the colonial era and extended post-independence often disregarded the traditional rights of forest-dwelling communities. The designation of forests as state property restricted access to essential resources like firewood, medicinal plants, and livelihood options. Despite the implementation of the Forest Rights Act (2006) in India, which sought to restore these rights, many communities still face eviction and harassment due to poor implementation, bureaucratic delays, and conflicts with conservation goals.

Land policies, too, have disproportionately affected marginalized populations. Historically, land ownership in many countries, including India, has been skewed along caste and class lines, leaving Dalits, tribal groups, and lower socio-economic classes without land or with insecure tenure. Even where land reform policies have been enacted to redistribute land and provide ownership rights, implementation has often been weak. Corruption, lack of political will, and manipulation by local elites have prevented land from reaching those who need it most. As a result, many marginalized communities remain trapped in cycles of poverty and dependence, lacking the basic security that land ownership provides.

Revenue policies, especially those related to taxation and land registration, often create further barriers for marginalized groups. Complex procedures, high registration fees, and lack of documentation disproportionately affect those with limited education or access to legal support. Revenue policies have sometimes facilitated the transfer of land from tribal or rural communities to corporations under the guise of development projects. In many cases, these policies contribute to land dispossession, forced migration, and the loss of cultural identity for indigenous populations. Moreover, revenue generated from mineral-rich lands, often located in tribal areas, rarely benefits the local communities themselves.

In response, some progressive legal frameworks have emerged that attempt to protect the rights of marginalized groups. These include the Panchayats (Extension to Scheduled Areas) Act (PESA), the Land Acquisition Act (2013), and the Forest Rights Act (2006). While these laws provide a legal basis for protecting land and forest rights, their effectiveness depends on active community participation, political will, and accountability mechanisms. Without sustained efforts to ensure justice and inclusion in policymaking and enforcement, forest, land, and revenue policies will continue to deepen the marginalization of vulnerable populations rather than alleviate it. Forest, land, and revenue policies have significantly impacted marginalized communities in India, particularly tribal populations. Here's a breakdown of the key policies and their effects:

Forest Policies

Pre-Colonial Period: Tribals had customary rights over forest resources, with village communities, zamindars, and governments sharing authority.

British Era (1865-1947): The British government introduced policies that asserted state monopoly over forests, restricting tribal access and commercializing forest resources.

Key policies include:

(a) *Forest Act of 1865:* Regulated Forest produce and asserted state control.

(b) *Forest Act of 1878:* Divided forests into reserved, protected, and village forests, tightening government control.

(c) *Forest Policy Resolution of 1894:* Prioritized state interests over people's interests, restricting tribal access.

Post-Independence (1952): The National Forest Policy prioritized national development over tribal rights, further restricting access to forest resources.

1988 Forest Policy: Introduced joint forest management, associating tribals in forest protection and development.

Impact on Tribal Communities

- **Loss of customary rights:** Tribals lost control over forest resources and were forced to adapt to new regulations.
- **Displacement and eviction:** Tribals were evicted from their lands, leading to displacement and loss of livelihood.
- **Exploitation:** Forest officials exploited tribals, using their power arbitrarily.
- **Limited access to resources:** Tribals faced restricted access to forest resources, affecting their livelihood and sustenance.

Land and Revenue Policies

- **Land alienation:** Tribals faced land alienation due to policies favouring non-tribal interests.

- **Revenue policies:** Revenue policies often prioritized state revenue over tribal welfare.

Recommendations and Reforms

- **Committee on Forests and Tribals (1982):** Recommended recognizing tribal rights and associating them in forest management.
- **Panchayats Extension to Scheduled Areas (PESA) Act (1996):** Decentralized Forest governance, recognizing tribal rights over community resources.
- **Recognition of tribal rights:** Efforts to recognize and protect tribal rights over forest resources and land.

Overall, forest, land, and revenue policies have had a profound impact on marginalized communities in India, often prioritizing state interests over tribal welfare. Efforts to recognize and protect tribal rights are crucial for promoting inclusive and sustainable development.

DEVELOPMENT IMPACT ON TRIBALS WITH SPECIAL REFERENCE TO KERALA

Development initiatives, while aimed at economic progress and modernization, have often had adverse effects on tribal communities, particularly in states like Kerala where indigenous populations inhabit ecologically sensitive and resource-rich regions. In Kerala, tribes such as the Paniyas, Kurichiyas, Adiyas, and Kattunaikkans primarily depend on forests and traditional agriculture for their livelihood. However, large-scale development projects, including dam construction, infrastructure expansion, and plantation agriculture, have led to the displacement of tribal populations from their ancestral lands. These projects have disrupted traditional lifestyles, uprooted cultural practices, and limited access to forests, which are central to the identity and sustenance of tribal communities in Kerala.

Despite Kerala's relatively high human development indicators, tribal communities in the state continue to lag behind in education, healthcare, and income levels. Displacement due to development projects has often not been accompanied by adequate rehabilitation or compensation. Many tribal families have been forced to resettle in non-agricultural or ecologically unsuitable areas, where they struggle with unemployment and food insecurity. Additionally, the alienation of land through fraudulent transactions or legal loopholes has exacerbated tribal marginalization. Development policies, though well-intentioned in some cases, often fail to consider the unique socio-cultural and ecological relationship that tribes have with their environment.

In recent years, there has been a growing recognition of the need for inclusive and sustainable development that respects tribal rights. The implementation of the Forest Rights Act (2006) in Kerala has provided some legal protection to tribal communities, allowing them to claim individual and community rights over forest land. However, challenges remain in terms of bureaucratic delays, limited awareness among tribal populations, and opposition from forest and revenue departments. For development to be truly equitable, policies must be participatory, culturally sensitive, and tailored to the needs and aspirations of tribal communities. Only then can development serve as a tool for empowerment rather than exclusion.

SCHEDULED CASTES AND SCHEDULED TRIBES: POLICIES AND THE ROLE OF PANCHAYATI RAJ INSTITUTIONS

Scheduled Castes (SCs) and Scheduled Tribes (STs) have long been subjected to systemic social discrimination, economic deprivation, and political exclusion in India. To rectify historical injustices and promote inclusive development, the Indian Constitution guarantees a range of safeguards for SCs and STs. Key policies include reservations in education, employment, and legislature; legal protections through the SC/ST (Prevention of Atrocities) Act, 1989; and various welfare schemes aimed at economic empowerment, education, and health. These measures seek to bridge the gap between these communities and the rest of society by ensuring access to opportunities and protection from discrimination and violence.

The 73rd Constitutional Amendment Act, 1992, Institutionalized the Panchayati Raj system, which marked a significant step toward grassroots democracy and empowerment of marginalized groups. The Act mandates the reservation of seats for SCs and STs in all three tiers of Panchayati Raj Institutions (PRIs)Gram Panchayat, Panchayat Samiti, and Zila Parishad. This provision ensures direct participation of these communities in local self-governance and decision-making processes. As elected representatives, SC and ST members can voice community-specific concerns, influence resource allocation, and contribute to the planning and implementation of development projects that address their needs.

In Scheduled Areas predominantly inhabited by tribal populations, the Panchayats (Extension to Scheduled Areas) Act (PESA), 1996, provides additional powers to local self-governments. PESA recognizes the traditional rights of tribal communities over natural resources and promotes self-governance through Gram Sabhas. Despite these constitutional provisions and policy frameworks, the actual impact of PRIs on SC/ST development depends on effective implementation, awareness among beneficiaries, and capacity-building efforts. Challenges like caste-based discrimination, lack of administrative support, and elite capture of institutions often hinder meaningful participation. Strengthening PRIs and ensuring accountability can transform them into powerful tools for inclusive governance and social justice for SCs and STs.Scheduled Castes (SCs) and Scheduled Tribes (STs) in India have been historically marginalized and disadvantaged groups. To address these disparities, the government has implemented various policies and schemes.

Constitutional Provisions

- **Article 341 and 342:** Define Scheduled Castes and Scheduled Tribes, respectively, and empower the President to specify these groups.
- **Article 17:** Abolishes untouchability, while Article 46 requires the State to promote the educational and economic interests of SCs and STs.
- **Article 330 and 332:** Provide for reservation of seats in the Lok Sabha and State Legislatures for SCs and STs.

Welfare Schemes

- **Pre-Matric Scholarship:** Financial assistance for pre-matric education to SC students.
- **Post Matric Scholarship for Scheduled Caste Students (PMS-SC):** Scholarship scheme for SC students pursuing higher education.
- **National Overseas Scholarship for SCs:** Financial assistance for SC students pursuing higher education abroad.
- **Rajiv Gandhi National Fellowship for SC Students:** Financial assistance for SC students pursuing research studies.
- **Special Central Assistance (SCA) to Scheduled Castes Sub-Plan (SCSP):** Targets financial and physical benefits for SCs.

Scheduled Tribes-specific Policies

- **Tribal Sub Plan (TSP) strategy:** Identifies problems and needs of tribal people, allocates resources, and prepares a policy framework for development.
- **Adivasi Mahila Sashaktikaran Yojana (AMSY):** Economic development scheme for ST women at concessional interest rates.
- **Digital Transformation of Tribal Schools:** Initiative to support digital transformation of schools for tribal students.
- **Eklavya Model Residential Schools (EMRS):** Scheme for model residential schools for tribal students.

Protective Laws

- **Protection of Civil Rights Act, 1955:** Penalizes offenses related to untouchability.

- **Scheduled Castes and the Scheduled Tribes (Prevention of Atrocities) Act, 1989:** Prevents atrocities against SCs and STs.
- **Prohibition of Employment as Manual Scavengers and their Rehabilitation Act, 2013:** Prohibits manual scavenging and provides for rehabilitation.

Role of Panchayati Raj Institutions

Panchayati Raj Institutions (PRIs) play a significant role in promoting the welfare and empowerment of Scheduled Castes (SCs) and Scheduled Tribes (STs) in India. Here's how:

Key Provisions

- **Reservation of Seats:** PRIs have reserved seats for SCs and STs in proportion to their population, ensuring representation in decision-making bodies.
- **Leadership Roles:** Reservation is also provided for offices of Chairpersons, enabling SCs and STs to hold leadership positions.

Empowerment through Participation

- **Decision-Making:** PRIs enable SCs and STs to participate in political decision-making, promoting their interests and needs.
- **Gram Sabha Meetings:** Mandatory Gram Sabha meetings provide a platform for SCs and STs to voice their concerns and participate in planning and implementation of development programs.

Functions and Responsibilities

- **Social Justice:** PRIs work towards social justice, addressing issues like untouchability and promoting equality.
- **Economic Development:** They implement schemes for economic development, such as poverty alleviation programs, and provide basic services like healthcare, education, and sanitation.
- **Welfare Schemes:** PRIs implement welfare schemes specifically for SCs and STs, promoting their socio-economic empowerment.

Challenges and Opportunities

- **Effective Implementation:** PRIs face challenges in effectively implementing policies and schemes for SCs and STs, requiring strengthening of institutions and capacity building.
- **Social Audit:** Regular social audits can help ensure transparency and accountability in PRI functioning, promoting better outcomes for SCs and STs.

- Overall, PRIs have the potential to significantly contribute to the empowerment and welfare of SCs and STs, but effective implementation and capacity building are crucial to achieving this goal.

CONCLUSION

The issue of marginalization is deeply embedded in the historical, social, and economic structures of societies worldwide. Both Western and Eastern ideologies have provided meaningful frameworks for understanding and challenging marginalization. The ideas of Karl Marx, focusing on economic class and capitalist exploitation, and Paulo Freire, emphasizing education as a tool for liberation, offer critical perspectives on the systemic nature of exclusion. These theories highlight that marginalization is not incidental but structurally produced and maintained, requiring conscious efforts toward transformation. Eastern ideologies, while varied, also converge on the need for social justice and equality. Mahatma Gandhi's philosophy of non-violence and upliftment of the oppressed emphasized a moral responsibility toward the most marginalized. He envisioned a society where everyone, regardless of caste or class, would have dignity and purpose. Swami Vivekananda stressed spiritual and educational empowerment, particularly for the poor, advocating for inner awakening and social reform as interlinked pathways to progress. Dr. B.R. Ambedkar's contributions stand out for their systemic and legal approach to marginalization, particularly of Dalits and other oppressed communities. His insistence on constitutional safeguards, representation, and equal opportunities brought a transformative vision to India's socio-political structure. Unlike Gandhi, Ambedkar emphasized structural change over moral persuasion, which was reflected in the incorporation of affirmative action policies and the enshrinement of equality in the Indian Constitution.

Marginalized groups possess inherent and inalienable rights that must be recognized to ensure their full inclusion in society. These rights include the right to exist without fear, to be free from discrimination, to maintain their cultural, religious, and linguistic identities, and to actively participate in public and political life. Without the protection and promotion of these rights, marginalization continues to reproduce cycles of poverty, exclusion, and inequality.Despite constitutional guarantees and legal frameworks, the practical realization of these rights remains a challenge. Discrimination in everyday life, barriers to education and employment, and lack of representation in decision-making bodies hinder the empowerment of marginalized communities. The translation of rights into lived realities requires not only laws and policies but also a fundamental shift in social attitudes and power structures. Forest, land, and revenue policies have played a significant role in the disempowerment of tribal communities. Often, these policies have prioritized national development and resource extraction over the rights and needs of indigenous populations. The alienation of land and denial of traditional rights have not only undermined the socio-economic fabric of tribal life but also eroded cultural identities. Policy frameworks must, therefore, be reoriented to respect and protect the rights of these communities, Integrating development with ecological and social justice.

The experience of Kerala provides an important lens to understand the complexities of tribal marginalization in a state that otherwise boasts high human development indicators. While the state has made commendable progress in literacy and health, tribal populations remain outside the mainstream in many respects. Issues such as displacement, poor access to quality education, and unemployment continue to plague tribal areas. Targeted interventions and localized governance reforms are essential to bridge this gap.The role of Scheduled Castes and Scheduled Tribes in the development narrative has gained legal recognition through reservation policies and special schemes. Yet, real empowerment depends on active participation and representation in governance processes. The Panchayati Raj system offers a platform for such engagement, and reservations in local bodies have indeed brought marginalized voices into decision-making. However, structural inequalities, lack of awareness, and interference from dominant groups often reduce these efforts to symbolic representation.To ensure meaningful participation and empowerment, Panchayati Raj Institutions must be strengthened through capacity-building, transparency, and community mobilization. When empowered, local governments can become vehicles of social justice, channelling resources and policies in ways that reflect the needs of marginalized communities. This grassroots approach holds the potential for more inclusive and context-sensitive development.

In conclusion, the path toward an inclusive society lies in a sustained commitment to both ideological understanding and practical implementation. Drawing on diverse perspectives—from Marx and Freire to Gandhi, Ambedkar, and Vivekananda—helps us grasp the multifaceted nature of marginalization and the importance of education, social reform, and political empowerment. Policies must be crafted and evaluated through a rights-based lens, ensuring that the voices of the marginalized are not only heard but also shape the future of our democratic and pluralistic societies.

KEY POINTS

- **Western and Eastern Perspectives on Marginalization:** Western ideologies like those of Karl Marx and Paulo Freire focus on class struggle and educational empowerment, while Eastern thinkers like Gandhi, Ambedkar, and Vivekananda addressed marginalization through moral reform, legal rights, and spiritual upliftment.

- **Rights of Marginalized Groups:** Marginalized communities are entitled to fundamental rights such as dignity, non-discrimination, cultural identity, and participation in public life, though these rights are often undermined by systemic barriers.
- **Forest, Land, and Revenue Policies:** Historically, these policies have dispossessed tribal and rural communities. Although reforms like the Forest Rights Act exist, their implementation remains inconsistent.
- **Development Impact on Tribals in Kerala:** Development projects have led to displacement and cultural erosion among Kerala's tribal communities, highlighting the need for inclusive and sensitive planning.
- **Policies for Scheduled Castes and Scheduled Tribes:** Affirmative action in education, employment, and politics aims to uplift SCs and STs, but social exclusion and implementation gaps still persist.
- **Role of Panchayati Raj Institutions:** PRIs have increased representation for marginalized groups at the local level, yet their impact is often limited by social and political challenges.

REFERENCES

1. Ambedkar, B.R. (2014). *Annihilation of Caste: The Annotated Critical Edition* (S. Anand, Ed.). Verso Books. (Original Work Published 1936)
2. Baviskar, A. (2004). *In the Belly of the River: Tribal Conflicts over Development in the Narmada Valley*. Oxford University Press.
3. Bijoy, C.R. (2003). The Adivasis of Kerala: A History of Resistance and Exclusion. *Indigenous Affairs*, 1(03), 38-45.
4. Brah, A. (1996). *Cartographies of Diaspora: Contesting Identities*. Routledge.
5. Dreze, J., & Sen, A. (2013). *An Uncertain Glory: India and its Contradictions*. Princeton University Press.
6. Fredman, S. (2011). *Discrimination Law*. Oxford University Press.
7. Freire, P. (2000). *Pedagogy of the Oppressed* (30th Anniversary ed., M.B. Ramos, Trans.). Bloomsbury. (Original Work Published 1970)
8. Gandhi, M.K. (2001). *The Essential Gandhi: An Anthology of his Writings on his Life, Work, and Ideas* (L. Fischer, Ed.). Vintage Books.
9. George, K. T., & Krishnaprasad, S. (2006). *Tribal Development in Kerala: A Critical Review.* Kerala Research Programme on Local Level Development, Centre for Development Studies.
10. Government of India. (1989). *The Scheduled Castes and Scheduled Tribes (Prevention of Atrocities) Act*. Ministry of Law and Justice. https://legislative.gov.in

11. Government of India. (1992). *The Constitution (Seventy-Third Amendment) Act, 1992*. Ministry of Panchayati Raj. https://panchayat.gov.in/
12. Government of India. (1996). *The Panchayats (Extension to Scheduled Areas) Act*. Ministry of Tribal Affairs. https://tribal.nic.in/
13. Government of India. (2006). *The Scheduled Tribes and Other Traditional Forest Dwellers (Recognition of Forest Rights) Act*. Ministry of Tribal Affairs. https://tribal.nic.in/
14. Government of India. (2013). *The Right to Fair Compensation and Transparency in Land Acquisition, Rehabilitation and Resettlement Act, 2013*. https://legislative.gov.in/
15. Human Rights Watch. (2020). *World Report 2020: Events of 2019*. Seven Stories Press.
16. Jha, S.N., & Mathur, P.C. (1999). *Decentralization and Local Politics*. Sage Publications.
17. Levien, M. (2018). *Dispossession without Development: Land Grabs in Neoliberal India*. Oxford University Press.
18. Marx, K., & Engels, F. (2002). *The Communist Manifesto*. Penguin Classics. (Original Work Published 1848)
19. Mathew, G. (1994). *Panchayati Raj: From Legislation to Movement*. Concept Publishing Company.
20. Menon, A.S. (2007). *A Survey of Kerala History*. DC Books.
21. Mohanty, B. (2001). Land Distribution among Scheduled Castes and Scheduled Tribes. *Economic and Political Weekly*, 36(40), 3857-3868.
22. Mosse, D. (2003). *The Rule of Water: Statecraft, Ecology, and Collective Action in South India*. Oxford University Press.
23. Nossiter, T.J. (1982). *Communism in Kerala: A Study in Political Adaptation*. University of California Press.
24. Rajkumar, A. (2011). *Religious Rights of Minorities in India*. Oxford University Press.
25. Raman, K.R. (2010). Development, Displacement and Resistance: The Law and the Rights of Indigenous People in Post-colonial India. *Sociological Bulletin*, 59(2), 228-245.
26. Sen, A. (1999). *Development as Freedom*. Oxford University Press.
27. Sen, A. (2009). *The Idea of Justice*. Harvard University Press.
28. Sengupta, M., & Patel, S. (2013). *Education and Marginalization: Towards Inclusive Education Policies in India*. Sage Publications.
29. Singh, S. (2008). PESA, the Forest Rights Act, and Tribal Rights in India: A Review. *Economic and Political Weekly*, 43(9), 18-21.
30. Skutnabb-Kangas, T. (2000). *Linguistic Genocide in Education—or Worldwide Diversity and Human Rights?* Lawrence Erlbaum Associates.
31. Sreekantan Nair, K. (1987). *Ayyankali: A Dalit Leader of Organic Protest*. Kerala Historical Society.

32. Subrahmanian, R. (2005). Education Exclusion and the Development State. *Compare: A Journal of Comparative and International Education*, 35(4), 439-455. https://doi.org/10.1080/03057920500331460
33. Sundar, N. (2017). *The Identity of a Dalit in Postcolonial India: Perspectives from Cultural Studies*. Oxford University Press.
34. Thorat, S., & Newman, K.S. (2010). *Blocked by Caste: Economic Discrimination in Modern India*. Oxford University Press.
35. Thornberry, P. (2002). *Indigenous Peoples and Human Rights*. Manchester University Press.
36. Tobin, J. (2013). The Rights of Indigenous Peoples and the Protection of their Identity. *Human Rights Quarterly*, 35(3), 484-502. https://doi.org/10.1353/hrq.2013.0049
37. United Nations. (1948). *Universal Declaration of Human Rights*. https://www.un.org/en/universal-declaration-human-rights/
38. United Nations. (1960). *Convention against Discrimination in Education*. https://www. ohchr. org/en/professionalinterest/ pages/ discrimination ineducation.aspx
39. United Nations. (1965). *International Convention on the Elimination of All Forms of Racial Discrimination*. https://www.ohchr.org/en/instruments-mechanisms/instruments/international-convention-elimination-all-forms-racial
40. United Nations. (2006). *Convention on the Rights of Persons with Disabilities*. https://www.un.org/development/desa/disabilities/convention-on-the-rights-of-persons-with-disabilities.html
41. United Nations. (2007). *United Nations Declaration on the Rights of Indigenous Peoples*. https://www.un.org/development/desa/indigenouspeoples/declaration-on-the-rights-of-indigenous-peoples.html
42. United Nations. (2007). *Universal Declaration on Bioethics and Human Rights*. https://www.unesco.org/en/biethics
43. Vivekananda, S. (2007). *Selections from the Complete Works of Swami Vivekananda*. Advaita Ashrama.
44. Young, I. M. (2000). *Inclusion and Democracy*. Oxford University Press.

3 CHAPTER

Problems and Challenges faced by Marginalized Groups

INTRODUCTION

Marginalization manifests in multiple interconnected forms, deeply impacting individuals and communities across social, environmental, political, educational, and economic dimensions. Vulnerable groupsespecially children often experience systematic exclusion from mainstream society, resulting in long-term disadvantage and limited access to essential rights and opportunities. This reality calls for a comprehensive understanding of the problems, challenges, and potential strategies to promote inclusion, equity, and justice. Social exploitation remains one of the most persistent challenges, with caste, ethnicity, gender, and class playing significant roles in maintaining unequal power structures. Marginalized individuals are often subjected to discrimination and exclusion in their daily lives, which restricts their social mobility and reinforces cycles of poverty and oppression. These structures also create barriers to accessing health, education, and employment. Environmental exploitation, particularly in rural and tribal areas, results from extractive development practices that deprive communities of their land, forest, and water resources. Displacement due to infrastructure projects, deforestation, and pollution affects not just livelihoods but also cultural heritage and identity. The lack of ecological justice disproportionately burdens the poor and marginalized.

Political marginalization involves the denial of agency, representation, and voice in decision-making processes. Policies may be enacted without the consultation of the affected communities, reinforcing their sense of powerlessness. Children from marginalized groups often grow up in environments where their families have limited influence in governance or policy implementation, perpetuating intergenerational inequality.Education, a key driver of empowerment, is both a site of exclusion and a tool for transformation. Children from marginalized backgrounds often attend poorly resourced schools, face language barriers, and are exposed to biased or irrelevant curricula. Discrimination by peers and teachers, along with a lack of culturally responsive pedagogy, further alienates them from formal education. Economic exploitation takes various forms underemployment, bonded labour, and denial of minimum wages. For children, this translates into child labour, trafficking, and even child soldiering in conflict zones. The loss of childhood and education in such cases limits their future prospects and sustains the cycle of poverty and marginalization.Child abuse and sexual exploitation, often underreported, affect children in vulnerable contexts with devastating consequences. These forms of violence are both a cause and result of marginalization, exacerbated by poverty, weak legal frameworks, and lack of social support. Victims often suffer in silence due to stigma and lack of access to justice.

In response, the government has introduced various schemes and policies aimed at promoting social and educational inclusion. Programs such as Sarva Shiksha Abhiyan, Right to Education Act, and mid-day meal schemes aim to ensure universal access to education and address socio-economic disparities. However, implementation gaps and structural inequalities often limit their effectiveness. Multi-cultural education and multi-grade teaching are critical strategies, especially in rural and diverse contexts. These approaches recognize the heterogeneity of student backgrounds and promote inclusive pedagogies that validate multiple identities. Such models are essential in classrooms where one teacher handles different grades and linguistic or cultural diversities.

To address these challenges, schools must be organized and managed with an inclusive vision. This includes developing teaching-learning materials that reflect cultural diversity, addressing language issues, and eliminating textbook biases. The hidden curriculum, often laden with stereotypes and normative assumptions, must be critically examined to foster an educational environment that respects and supports all learners.

CHALLENGES AND FORMS OF EXPLOITATION FACED BY MARGINALIZED GROUPS

Marginalized communities often face interconnected forms of exploitation and exclusion rooted in deep-seated social hierarchies and systemic inequalities. Social challenges include caste-based discrimination, gender bias, and stigmatization based on ethnicity or disability. These social divisions lead to exclusion from mainstream opportunities and restrict access to basic rights such as housing, healthcare, and justice. Women and children in these communities are particularly vulnerable, often facing violence, trafficking, and social invisibility. In many rural or tribal areas, social marginalization translates into isolation from infrastructure and basic services.

Environmental challenges disproportionately affect marginalized groups, especially indigenous and tribal communities. Forest-dwelling populations often face displacement due to large-scale development projects like dams, mining, and deforestation, resulting in loss of livelihood and cultural erosion. These groups, reliant on natural resources, rarely have legal ownership of the land they inhabit. Environmental degradation, climate change, and poor waste management in slums further worsen living conditions for the urban poor, exposing them to health hazards and environmental injustice.

In the political and educational spheres, marginalized groups often remain underrepresented. Despite constitutional provisions, real political participation is hindered by illiteracy, social intimidation, and lack of awareness. In education, systemic neglect, language barriers, and a lack of inclusive infrastructure prevent many from accessing quality schooling. Children from poor and marginalized families often drop out of school to work, becoming victims of child labour or even recruited as child soldiers in conflict zones. The lack of safe and inclusive learning environments also contributes to early marriages, especially for girls.

Economic exploitation is another critical issue. Members of marginalized communities often work in informal sectors with no job security, legal protections, or fair wages. Practices such as bonded labour, forced labour, and underpayment are common. Women are especially affected, often earning less than their male counterparts and facing workplace harassment. In some areas, exploitative landlords and employers maintain feudal control over marginalized populations, perpetuating cycles of poverty and dependence.

The exploitation of children through child abuse, child labour, child soldiering, and sexual violenceis one of the most tragic outcomes of marginalization. Poverty, lack of education, and broken social systems push children into hazardous labour or expose them to trafficking and abuse. Forced labour, both in domestic and industrial settings, remains a grim reality for many. Efforts by governments and NGOs have shown progress in some areas, but enforcement of child protection laws and rehabilitation programs often fall short, especially in remote or conflict-affected regions. Ending these abuses requires coordinated legal, social, and educational interventions that target both immediate risks and the underlying causes of marginalization.

SOCIAL CHALLENGES

Marginalized groups face persistent social exclusion and discrimination, which manifest in everyday life through limited access to social services, public spaces, and equal treatment. Caste, class, ethnicity, religion, gender, and disability often determine a person's place in the social hierarchy, especially in societies like India where traditional structures still influence social behaviour. This results in stigmatization, stereotyping, and segregation that deny these individuals dignity and equal opportunities. Women, Dalits, tribal groups, persons with disabilities, and sexual minorities are especially vulnerable to systemic discrimination, violence, and social invisibility.

Social marginalization also leads to limited participation in community decision-making and a lack of representation in social institutions. Those affected often live in isolated or underdeveloped areas where basic infrastructure, healthcare, and education are inadequate or absent. As a result, they become trapped in cycles of social dependency and are unable to assert their rights. This exclusion not only hampers their individual development but also weakens the fabric of society as a whole, perpetuating divisions and preventing inclusive growth.

- **Social exclusion:** Marginalized groups face exclusion from mainstream society, limiting their access to resources and opportunities.
- **Caste-based discrimination:** Caste systems can perpetuate social hierarchies, leading to discrimination and marginalization.
- **Gender-based violence:** Women and girls often face violence and discrimination, limiting their empowerment and participation.

ENVIRONMENTAL CHALLENGES

Marginalized communities, particularly indigenous and tribal groups, are among the most affected by environmental degradation and displacement. Large-scale development projects such as dams, mining operations, and deforestation often occur on lands inhabited by these communities, leading to forced evictions without adequate compensation or rehabilitation. These populations rely heavily on natural resources for their livelihoodforests for food, fuel, and medicine, and rivers for agriculture and daily use. When these resources are depleted or taken over for commercial exploitation, communities lose not just their economic foundation but also their cultural and spiritual connection to the land.

Environmental hazards such as pollution, climate change, and inadequate sanitation also disproportionately affect marginalized populations, especially in urban slums and rural peripheries. These areas often lack proper waste management, clean water, and resilient infrastructure, making residents more vulnerable to diseases and disasters. Additionally, marginalized groups usually have little say in environmental policy-making and are rarely consulted during environmental assessments, despite bearing the brunt of ecological risks. This exclusion further reinforces their vulnerability and deepens environmental injustice.

- **Deforestation and land degradation:** Unsustainable practices can lead to environmental degradation, affecting livelihoods and ecosystems.
- **Climate change:** Climate change exacerbates existing social and economic vulnerabilities, particularly for marginalized communities.
- **Resource exploitation:** Overexploitation of natural resources can lead to environmental degradation and social injustice.

POLITICAL CHALLENGES

Marginalized groups often suffer from political underrepresentation and exclusion in decision-making processes. Despite constitutional provisions for inclusive governance, such as reserved seats in legislatures and local bodies, many individuals from these communities face systemic barriers that prevent them from exercising their political rights. Illiteracy, lack of awareness, fear of intimidation, and historical disenfranchisement limit their ability to vote, run for office, or influence policy. As a result, their concerns are frequently overlooked, and policies fail to address their specific needs or circumstances.

Additionally, political structures may reinforce existing inequalities through biased implementation of laws and development schemes. Corruption, bureaucratic delays, and lack of accountability often obstruct marginalized communities from accessing government welfare programs and legal protections. In many cases, local elites dominate political institutions, silencing dissent and excluding alternative voices. This political marginalization not only weakens democracy but also perpetuates social and economic disparities, making it difficult for these communities to advocate for justice and sustainable development.

- **Lack of representation:** Marginalized groups often lack representation in decision-making processes, limiting their influence on policies affecting their lives.
- **Discrimination and bias:** Institutional biases and discriminatory practices can perpetuate marginalization.
- **Limited access to justice:** Marginalized groups may face barriers in accessing justice, exacerbating existing social and economic inequalities.

EDUCATIONAL CHALLENGES

Educational challenges remain a significant barrier for marginalized groups such as Scheduled Castes, Scheduled Tribes, minority communities, and economically weaker sections. These communities often face systemic exclusion due to poverty, social discrimination, and lack of access to quality educational institutions. In rural and tribal areas, schools may be understaffed, poorly equipped, or located far from students' homes, making regular attendance difficult. Additionally, language barriers and culturally irrelevant curricula can alienate students, leading to high dropout rates and poor academic performance. Girls from marginalized backgrounds face further obstacles due to gender norms, early marriage, and safety concerns.

The impact of these challenges is long-lasting, contributing to intergenerational cycles of poverty and exclusion. Lack of quality education reduces opportunities for gainful employment and participation in civic life, reinforcing social hierarchies and economic inequality. Although government schemes like mid-day meals, scholarships, and Right to Education (RTE) have helped improve enrolment, the gap in learning outcomes persists. Addressing these issues requires inclusive policies, better infrastructure, teacher training, community involvement, and curriculum reforms that reflect the diverse experiences of marginalized groups.

- **Limited access to education:** Marginalized groups often face barriers in accessing quality education, limiting their opportunities for social mobility.
- **Discrimination in education:** Educational institutions can perpetuate existing social hierarchies, leading to discrimination and marginalization.
- **Lack of inclusive curricula:** Curricula may not reflect the experiences and perspectives of marginalized groups, limiting their sense of belonging and identity.

ECONOMIC EXPLOITATION

Economic exploitation is a major issue affecting marginalized groups such as Dalits, Adivasis, migrant workers, and minority communities, who are often relegated to low-paying, insecure, and informal sector jobs. These individuals are frequently denied fair wages, safe working conditions, and social security benefits. Due to a lack of education and limited access to capital or skill development, many are forced into bonded labour, daily wage work, or other exploitative economic arrangements. Caste-based occupations and systemic discrimination further restrict their economic mobility, trapping entire communities in cycles of poverty.

The structural nature of economic exploitation is reinforced by unequal access to resources like land, credit, and markets. For example, tribal communities are often displaced by development projects without adequate compensation or rehabilitation, leading to loss of livelihoods. Women from marginalized groups face double discrimination earning less than their male counterparts while also bearing the burden of unpaid domestic work. Despite the presence of constitutional safeguards and welfare schemes, poor implementation and corruption often prevent the benefits from reaching the intended recipients. Empowering marginalized groups economically requires targeted policies, inclusive financial systems, and strong legal enforcement of labour rights.

- **Poverty and inequality:** Marginalized groups often face significant economic challenges, including poverty and limited access to resources.
- **Exploitation:** Marginalized groups may be vulnerable to exploitation, including forced labour and child labour.
- **Limited access to employment opportunities:** Marginalized groups may face barriers in accessing employment opportunities, limiting their economic mobility.

CHILD ABUSE

Child abuse remains a severe and pervasive issue, particularly among marginalized and vulnerable communities. Children living in poverty, broken families, or conflict zones are at heightened risk of physical, emotional, and sexual abuse. These children often lack access to safe environments, proper care, and legal protection, making them easy targets for abusers. In many cases, the abuse goes unreported due to fear, stigma, or lack of awareness about children's rights. The trauma from abuse can lead to long-term psychological harm, disrupted education, and reduced opportunities for growth and development.

In marginalized communities, institutional neglect and weak child protection systems exacerbate the problem. Schools, shelters, and even homes sometimes become unsafe spaces due to the absence of trained personnel and oversight. Societal norms that normalize corporal punishment or gender-based violence further perpetuate abuse. Additionally, due to low literacy and legal awareness, families may not recognize abuse or know how to seek help. Addressing child abuse requires a combination of legal enforcement, awareness campaigns, access to counselling, and strong community-based child protection mechanisms.

CHILD LABOUR

Child labour is a persistent challenge, especially among marginalized and economically disadvantaged communities. Driven by poverty, lack of access to quality education, and social norms, children are often forced to work from a young age to support their families. These children may be found working in agriculture, construction, domestic work, factories, and even hazardous industries like mining or fireworks production. Long working hours, physical strain, and exposure to unsafe conditions severely affect their health and development. As a result, many of these children are deprived of their right to education and a safe, nurturing childhood.

In marginalized societies, child labour is both a cause and consequence of systemic inequality. Families belonging to lower castes, tribal groups, or migrant communities often lack legal and social protection, making their children vulnerable to exploitation. In many cases, child labour becomes intergenerational, with parents and children trapped in cycles of low-income and informal work. Although laws like the Child Labour (Prohibition and Regulation) Act in India exist, enforcement is often weak, and loopholes allow continued exploitation. Combating child labour requires addressing its root causespoverty, lack of education, and social exclusion—through targeted interventions and community engagement.

CHILD SOLDIERING

Child soldiering is one of the gravest violations of children's rights, primarily occurring in conflict-affected regions. Marginalized children, particularly those from impoverished, displaced, or stateless communities, are the most vulnerable to recruitment by armed groups. These children are forcibly conscripted, abducted, or sometimes even volunteered by desperate families in exchange for basic necessities or protection. Once recruited, they are used not only as combatants but also as porters, spies, messengers, or subjected to sexual exploitation. The psychological and physical toll of such experiences is immense, leaving long-term trauma and disrupting the possibility of a normal life.

The challenge of reintegrating former child soldiers into society is compounded by stigma, lack of support systems, and the absence of education or livelihood opportunities. Many of these children return to communities where they are either feared or rejected, while others struggle with identity crises and post-traumatic stress. International conventions like the UN Convention on the Rights of the Child prohibit the use of children in armed conflict, and organizations such as UNICEF and various NGOs work on rehabilitation. However, political instability, poverty, and weak enforcement of child protection laws make it difficult to fully eliminate child soldiering. A holistic approach involving education, mental health care, community acceptance, and sustained peace-building efforts is essential to address this grave issue.

SEXUAL ABUSE

Sexual abuse is a widespread and deeply harmful issue, particularly affecting individuals from marginalized communities who often lack the power, protection, and voice to report or resist such violence. Women, children, people with disabilities, and members of LGBTQ+ groups are especially vulnerable due to their social and economic positions. In many cases, victims face abuse in familiar environments such as homes, schools, workplaces, or institutional settings, and are often silenced by fear, shame, or threats. The trauma caused by sexual abuse can have long-lasting impacts on physical health, mental well-being, and self-esteem, affecting victims' ability to lead safe and dignified lives.

In marginalized societies, systemic factors like poverty, illiteracy, and social stigma further complicate efforts to prevent and address sexual abuse. Victims may not have access to support services such as legal aid, medical care, or counselling, and often encounter victim-blaming attitudes from law enforcement or community members. Cultural norms and patriarchal beliefs may discourage survivors from speaking out, allowing perpetrators to go unpunished. Although there are legal protections in place, such as the Protection of Children from Sexual Offences (POCSO) Act in India, implementation remains inconsistent. A multifaceted approach involving education, community sensitization, strong legal enforcement, and survivor-centred support systems is vital to combat this issue effectively.

FORCED LABOUR

Forced labour is a severe violation of human rights, where individuals are coerced to work under threat, deception, or exploitation, often without the freedom to leave. This issue disproportionately affects marginalized communities, including Dalits, tribal groups, migrants, and impoverished families. In many cases, people are trapped in bonded labour systems, where debts are inherited across generations and used to justify exploitative work conditions. Victims of forced labour often endure long hours, unsafe environments, physical abuse, and lack of compensation, all while being denied basic dignity and legal protection.

Despite laws prohibiting such practices, enforcement is often weak, and exploiters take advantage of legal loopholes, corruption, and the silence of vulnerable populations. Women and children are especially susceptible to being trafficked for forced domestic work, agriculture, brick kilns, or even sexual exploitation. Illiteracy, poverty, and lack of awareness about rights make it difficult for victims to seek help or escape. Combating forced labour requires robust legal action, accessible support services for victims, economic empowerment initiatives, and community-level education to break the cycle of exploitation.Specific issues can be summarized as:

- **Child abuse:** Children in marginalized communities may face increased vulnerability to abuse and exploitation.
- **Child labour:** Children may be forced into labour, limiting their access to education and perpetuating cycles of poverty.
- **Child soldiering:** Children may be recruited into armed groups, exposing them to violence and trauma.
- **Sexual abuse:** Marginalized groups, particularly women and girls, may face increased vulnerability to sexual abuse and exploitation.
- **Forced labour:** Marginalized groups may be forced into labour, often under exploitative conditions.

SOCIAL AND EDUCATIONAL INCLUSION - GOVERNMENT SCHEMES AND POLICIES

Social and educational inclusion are central to India's efforts to uplift marginalized communities and bridge long-standing inequalities. Recognizing the deep-rooted challenges faced by Scheduled Castes (SCs), Scheduled Tribes (STs), Other Backward Classes (OBCs), minorities, and persons with disabilities, the government has launched several schemes aimed at fostering dignity, equality, and opportunity. Social inclusion initiatives like the Scheduled Castes Sub Plan (SCSP) and Tribal Sub Plan (TSP) channel targeted funds for welfare programs, housing, skill development, and livelihood support. These schemes aim to address historical discrimination and ensure the integration of excluded communities into mainstream development.

In the education sector, Right to Education (RTE) Act, 2009 marked a turning point by guaranteeing free and compulsory education for children aged 6 to 14 years. It mandates that 25% of seats in private unaided schools be reserved for children from economically weaker sections. This inclusion measure helps reduce educational disparities by bringing marginalized children into classrooms with better resources. Schemes such as Sarva Shiksha Abhiyan (SSA) and Rashtriya Madhyamik Shiksha Abhiyan (RMSA) further promote access, retention, and quality education, especially in rural and disadvantaged areas.

Special focus has also been placed on higher education through programs like Post-Matric Scholarships, National Overseas Scholarship, and Top-Class Education Scheme, which support SC/ST students in pursuing advanced studies in India and abroad. In addition, Eklavya Model Residential Schools have been established for tribal children to provide high-quality education in remote areas. Vocational training and digital learning initiatives like Skill India and PM e-Vidya help bridge the employability gap by equipping youth from marginalized backgrounds with practical skills.

Despite these efforts, challenges remain in implementation, especially in reaching remote regions and addressing dropout rates among girls and children with disabilities. Issues such as social stigma, lack of awareness, and infrastructural gaps hinder the full realization of inclusive goals. To strengthen impact, policies must be more participatory, involve community engagement, and focus on quality alongside access. True social and educational inclusion lies not only in enrolling students but also in creating a supportive and equitable environment where every individual can thrive.

The Indian government has implemented various schemes and policies to promote social and educational inclusion, focusing on marginalized communities, including Scheduled Castes (SCs), Scheduled Tribes (STs), minorities, women, and weaker sections. The Key Initiatives are as under:

- **Reservation Policy:** Ensures 27% reservation of seats for Other Backward Classes (OBCs) in central educational institutions.
- **Special Schemes:** The University Grants Commission (UGC) designs special schemes to address equity and inclusion for minorities, women, and weaker sections.
- **Empowerment of SCs:** The Department of Social Justice & Empowerment implements policies and programs for SC empowerment, including central sector schemes.
- **Inclusive Education:** Policies aim to improve educational opportunities for disadvantaged groups, including girls and children from SC and ST backgrounds.

Government Bodies

- **NITI Aayog's Social Justice & Empowerment Division:** Works on policies and programs for social inclusion, including SC empowerment and welfare of the aged.
- **Department of Social Justice & Empowerment:** Implements central sector schemes for SCs and other marginalized groups.

Challenges

- **Social Group Disparities:** Regions like Bihar, Jharkhand, Chhattisgarh, and parts of Odisha, Rajasthan, and Madhya Pradesh face significant disparities.
- **Cultural and Traditional Factors:** Social discrimination affects access to education for marginalized groups.

Objectives

- **Social Justice:** Achieve social justice through inclusive access to education and economic opportunities.

- **Economic Efficiency:** Promote economic efficiency by ensuring inclusive access to higher education.

MULTI-CULTURAL EDUCATION AND MULTI-GRADE TEACHING IN RURAL CONTEXT

Multicultural education is essential in rural contexts where classrooms often include children from diverse socio-cultural, linguistic, and economic backgrounds. In rural India, for instance, students may belong to various castes, tribal groups, or religious minorities, each with their own languages, traditions, and learning needs. Multicultural education aims to respect this diversity, promote inclusivity, and ensure that every child's identity is acknowledged and valued. It encourages teaching practices that integrate local culture, folk knowledge, and mother tongues into the curriculum, thereby improving student engagement and reducing dropout rates.

Multi-grade teachingwhere a single teacher handles students of different grades simultaneously is common in rural schools due to teacher shortages, limited infrastructure, and low student populations. While challenging, it can also be an opportunity to implement child-centred and peer-learning strategies. In multi-grade settings, teachers often group students by learning level rather than age or grade, allowing more personalized instruction. However, effective multi-grade teaching requires specific training, flexible curricula, and teaching-learning materials designed for such environments.

Integrating multicultural and multi-grade teaching approaches can enhance educational equity in rural settings. Culturally relevant pedagogy helps connect textbook knowledge to students' real-life experiences, making learning more meaningful. For example, stories, songs, and local histories can be used across grades to teach language and social science while reinforcing cultural pride. Moreover, when children from different backgrounds interact in inclusive settings, it fosters mutual respect, tolerance, and a stronger sense of community.

Despite the potential benefits, both multicultural education and multi-grade teaching face systemic challenges. Rural schools often lack adequate teacher training, resources, and administrative support. Rigid curricula and examination-focused systems can discourage teachers from adopting innovative or inclusive methods. To overcome these barriers, educational policy must prioritize investment in rural teacher education, provide multilingual materials, and develop monitoring frameworks tailored for diverse and multi-level learning environments.

In rural educational contexts, where diverse cultures, languages, and socio-economic backgrounds intersect, multi-cultural education and multi-grade teaching emerge as essential and complementary approaches to ensure inclusive and effective learning experiences. Multi-cultural education refers to an approach that values diversity, promotes inclusivity, and recognizes the unique experiences of diverse student populations. It fosters empathy and mutual understanding among students from different backgrounds, encourages critical thinking and problem-solving, and prepares learners for a globalized world. However, its implementation in rural areas is often challenged by limited resources, inadequate infrastructure, and the need for well-trained teachers capable of handling diverse classrooms. On the other hand, multi-grade teaching—where a single teacher instructs students from different grade levels in one classroom—is a practical solution in rural settings facing teacher shortages. This approach promotes flexible resource use, supports peer-to-peer learning, and enhances collaboration among students. Yet, it demands highly skilled teachers who can address varied learning needs and sustain student engagement across grades. In the rural context, educators must be culturally sensitive, respecting local traditions, languages, and community dynamics. Community involvement becomes vital, ensuring that educational practices align with the needs and values of the local population. Furthermore, resource constraints necessitate creativity in teaching methods and materials, while continuous professional development and support for teachers remain crucial. By thoughtfully integrating multi-cultural education and multi-grade teaching, educators can build inclusive, responsive, and dynamic classrooms that truly cater to the diverse needs of rural students.

ORGANIZATION AND MANAGEMENT OF SCHOOLS TO ADDRESS SOCIO-CULTURAL DIVERSITY

Addressing socio-cultural diversity in school organization and management is crucial for creating inclusive learning environments. Schools, particularly in multicultural societies like India, must recognize the varied cultural, linguistic, and social backgrounds of their students. Effective school management begins with acknowledging this diversity and creating policies that promote equity and inclusion. This includes forming school development plans that are sensitive to the needs of marginalized communities and ensuring that students from different castes, religions, tribes, and linguistic groups feel respected and represented.

A key strategy in managing socio-cultural diversity is recruiting a diverse teaching staff and offering regular professional development on inclusive pedagogy. Teachers trained to handle diversity are better equipped to use culturally relevant examples, address biases in textbooks, and respond to the specific needs of students from different communities. Language-sensitive policiessuch as introducing mother tongue instruction at the primary levelcan also improve learning outcomes and participation, especially among tribal and minority children.

Community involvement is another important aspect of inclusive school management. School Management Committees (SMCs) and Parent-Teacher Associations (PTAs) should include representatives from all social groups to ensure that decisions reflect the voices of marginalized populations. Regular interaction with local communities can help schools understand cultural practices, address attendance issues, and improve the overall learning environment. Initiatives like cultural days, multilingual assemblies, and inclusive school celebrations foster mutual respect and cultural pride among students.

However, challenges remain, such as systemic biases, lack of training, and underrepresentation of minorities in educational leadership. Schools often struggle with limited resources, large class sizes, and rigid curricula that may not allow flexibility for cultural adaptation. To overcome these, education policies must prioritize inclusive school leadership, provide adequate funding, and implement monitoring systems that assess inclusivity alongside academic performance. Only through conscious organizational changes can schools become truly inclusive institutions that prepare all children for an equitable society.Effective organization and management of schools can help address socio-cultural diversity by:

- **Inclusive Curriculum:** Developing curricula that reflect diverse cultures, languages, and experiences.
- **Culturally Responsive Teaching:** Teachers incorporating diverse perspectives and experiences into their teaching practices.
- **Diverse Staff:** Recruiting teachers and staff from diverse backgrounds to create a more inclusive environment.
- **Parent and Community Engagement:** Fostering partnerships with parents and local communities to promote understanding and support.
- **Professional Development:** Providing ongoing training and support for teachers to develop cultural competence.

School Leadership

- **Visionary Leadership:** School leaders promoting a vision of inclusivity and diversity.
- **Cultural Awareness:** Leaders understanding and valuing diverse cultures and experiences.
- **Inclusive Policies:** Developing policies that promote equity, diversity, and inclusion.

Challenges

- **Limited Resources:** Schools may face challenges in implementing inclusive practices due to limited resources.

- **Resistance to Change:** Some staff or community members may resist changes aimed at promoting diversity and inclusion.
- **Cultural and Linguistic Barriers:** Schools may need to navigate cultural and linguistic differences to effectively serve diverse student populations.

Best Practices

- **Collaboration:** Fostering collaboration among teachers, staff, parents, and community members.
- **Student-Centred Approach:** Prioritizing student needs and experiences in decision-making processes.
- **Ongoing Evaluation:** Regularly evaluating and refining policies and practices to ensure they promote diversity and inclusion.

By implementing these strategies, schools can create inclusive environments that value and support diverse student populations.

TEACHING-LEARNING PROCESSES AND SUPPORT MATERIALS ADDRESSING VARIOUS ASPECTS OF DIVERSITY IN EDUCATION

Teaching-learning processes play a vital role in ensuring that all children, regardless of background, can access meaningful and equitable education. In diverse classroomsespecially those found in rural or multicultural areasteachers must adopt inclusive pedagogies that cater to varied learning styles, linguistic backgrounds, and socio-cultural realities. Methods such as activity-based learning, group work, storytelling, and experiential learning not only make lessons engaging but also respect the lived experiences of marginalized students. Effective teaching includes differentiated instruction and continuous assessment strategies that respond to students' individual progress rather than applying a one-size-fits-all approach.

One major barrier to inclusive education is the language of instruction. In multilingual countries like India, children from tribal or non-dominant language communities often struggle when instruction is in a state or national language unfamiliar to them. Early education in a child's mother tongue is linked to better comprehension and retention, as supported by the National Education Policy (2020). Therefore, teaching-learning materials should be developed in local languages, and teachers must be trained in multilingual methodologies to bridge language gaps while supporting a smooth transition to second or third languages.

Another concern is bias in textbooks, which may reinforce stereotypes related to caste, gender, religion, or region. Many textbooks lack diverse representation, leading to the invisibility or misrepresentation of marginalized groups. Inclusive curriculum development involves critically reviewing textbooks to ensure balanced portrayals of various cultures, identities, and contributions. Teachers must also be equipped to identify and address bias in content and initiate discussions that encourage critical thinking and empathy among students.

In addition to formal curricula, co-curricular and extracurricular activities must be designed to support the diverse talents and needs of students. Activities such as drama, arts, sports, and cultural programs provide children from marginalized groups with platforms for self-expression and confidence building. These activities also foster social cohesion and help break down barriers of caste, class, and gender. Schools should encourage participation of all students by eliminating hidden costs and promoting an inclusive environment where every child feels valued and capable.

The hidden curriculumthe set of unwritten social and cultural messages students receive at schoolalso deeply affects learners. It includes the values conveyed through teacher attitudes, classroom interaction, discipline methods, and peer dynamics. For instance, favouring students from certain backgrounds, ignoring discriminatory remarks, or assigning lower expectations to marginalized children can perpetuate exclusion. Educators must be conscious of the hidden curriculum and actively promote respect, equity, and democratic values in their daily practices to ensure a truly inclusive education for all.

Teaching-Learning Processes and Support Materials

- **Inclusive Curriculum:** Developing curricula that reflect diverse cultures, languages, and experiences.
- **Language Support:** Providing language support for students who speak different languages or dialects.
- **Diverse Teaching Methods:** Using diverse teaching methods to cater to different learning styles and needs.
- **Support Materials:** Developing support materials that are inclusive, unbiased, and relevant to diverse student populations.

Addressing Language Issues

- **Language Barriers:** Identifying and addressing language barriers that may hinder student learning.
- **Multilingual Approach:** Using a multilingual approach to teaching and learning.
- **Language Support Programs:** Implementing language support programs for students who need additional help.

Bias in Textbooks

- **Inclusive Representation:** Ensuring that textbooks represent diverse cultures, languages, and experiences.
- **Avoiding Stereotypes:** Avoiding stereotypes and biases in textbook content.
- **Regular Review:** Regularly reviewing and updating textbooks to ensure they remain relevant and inclusive.

Curriculum and Curricular Activities

- **Diverse Curriculum:** Developing curricula that cater to diverse student needs and interests.
- **Inclusive Activities:** Incorporating inclusive activities that promote diversity, equity, and social justice.
- **Flexibility:** Providing flexibility in curricular activities to accommodate different learning styles and needs.

Hidden Curriculum

- **Implicit Messages:** Recognizing the implicit messages conveyed through school culture and practices.
- **Unintended Biases:** Identifying and addressing unintended biases in teaching practices and materials.
- **Promoting Inclusivity:** Promoting inclusivity and diversity through school culture and practices.

By addressing these aspects, educators can create inclusive learning environments that support the diverse needs of students.

CONCLUSION

Addressing the multifaceted problems and challenges faced by marginalized communities—especially childrenrequire a holistic and sustained approach. Social, environmental, political, educational, and economic exploitation continue to intersect, creating a web of disadvantage that undermines both individual potential and societal progress. Marginalized children are disproportionately affected, experiencing not only systemic discrimination but also various forms of abuse, such as child labour, child soldiering, and sexual exploitation.The persistence of child abuse and forced labour underscores the urgency for stronger protective mechanisms and proactive social interventions. These issues are deeply rooted in poverty, lack of awareness, and weak enforcement of laws. Effective child protection must therefore integrate legal, social, and educational strategies to prevent exploitation and rehabilitate victims. This is essential for creating a secure and nurturing environment where children can thrive.

Social and educational inclusion plays a pivotal role in breaking cycles of marginalization. Government schemes and policies, such as the Right to Education Act, Samagra Shiksha Abhiyan, and child welfare programs, have contributed to expanding access and improving infrastructure. However, the success of these initiatives depends on localized implementation, community involvement, and consistent monitoring to ensure they genuinely benefit the intended populations.Education must be responsive to the cultural, linguistic, and socio-economic realities of children. Multi-cultural education fosters respect for diversity and helps dismantle stereotypes and prejudices. By recognizing and validating different cultural identities within the curriculum, schools become spaces of empowerment rather than exclusion. Such inclusivity can play a transformative role in shaping young minds.

Multi-grade teaching, common in rural and under-resourced settings, must be supported with appropriate training and materials. Teachers should be equipped to handle diverse learning levels and backgrounds within a single classroom. When implemented effectively, multi-grade teaching not only makes education accessible but also encourages peer learning and cooperation among students.The organization and management of schools must evolve to meet the demands of a socially diverse student population. Inclusive school governance, community participation, and culturally aware leadership are essential for ensuring equity in education. School structures should be flexible, enabling innovations that address local needs while maintaining national standards.Language remains a critical barrier in education. Teaching-learning processes must accommodate the linguistic diversity of students by incorporating mother-tongue instruction in early years and offering multilingual support. This not only enhances comprehension but also affirms a child's identity and cultural roots, reducing alienation and dropout rates.

Textbooks and curriculum must be critically examined for biases and hidden messages that perpetuate inequality. Materials should reflect the lived realities of all children, especially those from marginalized groups. Inclusive content, free of stereotypes, allows students to see themselves in their learning journey and fosters a sense of belonging in the education system.Curricular and co-curricular activities must be designed to meet the diverse needs of children, providing space for expression, creativity, and social learning. Activities that encourage collaboration and respect across differences are vital for building inclusive school cultures. These experiences help students appreciate pluralism and develop skills necessary for democratic citizenship.

In conclusion, a just and equitable education system must move beyond access to address the deeper structural and systemic barriers that marginalize children. Through inclusive pedagogy, equitable policies, and community-centred school management, education can become a powerful tool for social transformation. Ensuring that every child, regardless of background, has the opportunity to learn, grow, and succeed is both a moral imperative and a foundation for sustainable development.

KEY POINTS

- **Problems and Challenges Faced by Children:** Children from marginalized communities face numerous forms of exploitation, including social, environmental, political, educational, and economic injustices. Specific threats such as child abuse, child labour, child soldiering, sexual abuse, and forced labour severely hinder their growth, safety, and rights.
- **Social and Educational Inclusion:** Government policies and schemes aim to promote social and educational inclusion for vulnerable children. These initiatives focus on providing equal access to quality education, protecting rights, and ensuring marginalized groups are not left behind in the development process.
- **Multi-cultural Education and Rural Teaching:** Multi-cultural education plays a vital role in acknowledging and respecting the diverse cultural backgrounds of students. In rural areas, multi-grade teaching is commonly practiced to efficiently manage limited resources and reach students from different age groups within the same classroom.
- **School Organization for Socio-cultural Diversity:** Effective school management is essential to accommodate socio-cultural diversity. Inclusive practices, flexible structures, and community engagement help build an environment where all students feel accepted and supported regardless of their background.
- **Teaching-Learning Processes and Language Issues:** Language barriers often obstruct learning for children from non-dominant linguistic groups. Addressing these issues through multilingual support and culturally responsive pedagogy enhances students' comprehension and participation in class.
- **Bias in Textbooks and Materials:** Textbooks and educational materials may contain biases that reinforce stereotypes or ignore the experiences of marginalized communities. Revising content to be inclusive and accurate helps foster mutual respect and critical awareness among learners.
- **Inclusive Curriculum and Activities:** Curricula must be designed to address the diverse needs of children. Culturally relevant content and inclusive co-curricular activities ensure that learning experiences resonate with all students and promote engagement.

- **Addressing the Hidden Curriculum:** The hidden curriculum—unspoken or implicit messages within the school culture—can perpetuate exclusion and inequality. Educators must be aware of these dynamics and work to ensure that all aspects of the school environment support inclusion and respect.

REFERENCES

1. Amnesty International. (2017). *The Plight of Sexually Abused Women and Children in Marginalized Communities*. https://www.amnesty.org/en/sexual-abuse
2. Apple, M.W. (2004). *Ideology and Curriculum* (3rd ed.). RoutledgeFalmer.
3. Banks, J.A. (2015). *Cultural Diversity and Education: Foundations, Curriculum, and Teaching* (6th ed.). Routledge.
4. Desai, A., & Shroff, P. (2016). *Exclusion and Inclusion: Marginalized Communities and Social Development in India*. Oxford University Press.
5. Govinda, R., & Josephine, Y. (2004). *Para Teachers in India: A Review*. National Institute of Educational Planning and Administration (NIEPA).
6. Government of India. (2009). *The Right of Children to Free and Compulsory Education Act, 2009*. Ministry of Education. https://www.education.gov.in
7. Government of India. (2020). *National Education Policy 2020*. Ministry of Education. https://www.education.gov.in
8. Human Rights Watch. (2020). *Child Soldiers: A Global Crisis*. https://www.hrw.org/report/2020/04/15/child-soldiers-global-crisis
9. International Labour Organization (ILO). (2019). *Forced Labour, Modern Slavery, and Human Trafficking: Global Trends*. https://www.ilo.org/global/statistics
10. ILO. (2019). *Child Labour: Global Estimates and Trends 2000-2016*. International Labour Organization. https://www.ilo.org/global/statistics-and-databases
11. Kumar, K. (2004). *What is worth teaching?* (3rd ed.). Orient BlackSwan.
12. Kumar, R., & Roy, K. (2017). Forced Labour and its Socio-economic Consequences in South Asia. *Journal of Human Rights*, 22(3), 101-113. https://doi.org/10.1080/10576622.2017.1190136
13. Little, A.W. (2006). *Education for All and Multi-grade Teaching: Challenges and Opportunities*. Springer. https://doi.org/10.1007/978-1-4020-4470-2
14. Ministry of Education. (2018). *Samagra Shiksha Abhiyan: An Integrated Scheme for School Education*. Government of India. https://www.education.gov.in/samagra-shiksha
15. Ministry of Social Justice and Empowerment. (2021). *Post-Matric Scholarship Scheme for SC Students*. Government of India. https://socialjustice.gov.in
16. Ministry of Tribal Affairs. (2020). *Eklavya Model Residential Schools*. Government of India. https://tribal.nic.in
17. Nambissan, G.B. (2009). *Exclusion and Discrimination in Schools: Experiences of Dalit Children*. Indian Institute of Dalit Studies and UNICEF.

18. Nanda, S., & Jain, A. (2016). Sexual Violence in Marginalized Communities: Causes and Solutions. *Feminist Review,* 19(2), 55-73. https://doi.org/10.1080/222123456.2016.1198765
19. NCERT. (2005). *National Curriculum Framework 2005.* National Council of Educational Research and Training. https://ncert.nic.in
20. NCERT. (2006). *National Curriculum Framework 2005: Position Paper on Curriculum, Syllabus and Textbooks.* National Council of Educational Research and Training. https://ncert.nic.in
21. NCERT. (2006). *National Curriculum Framework 2005: Position Paper on Education of Children with Special Needs.* National Council of Educational Research and Training. https://ncert.nic.in
22. Planning Commission. (2013). *Evaluation Study of the Special Component Plan for Scheduled Castes and Tribal Sub-Plan.* NITI Aayog. https://niti.gov.in
23. Sadker, D., & Zittleman, K. (2010). *Teachers, Schools, and Society: A Brief Introduction to Education* (2nd ed.). McGraw-Hill Education.
24. Sethi, M., & Anand, S. (2018). Children in Distress: Addressing Child Abuse in Marginalized Communities. *Journal of Child Protection,* 10(1), 12-24.
25. Sharma, A., & Mehta, K. (2017). Environmental Degradation and its Impact on Marginalized Communities. *Journal of Social Development,* 5(2), 45-58. https://doi.org/10.1080/123456789.2017.1245678
26. Sharma, S. (2018). *The Challenges of Poverty and Inequality: A Global Perspective.* Oxford University Press.
27. Singal, N. (2011). Addressing Diversity in Indian Education: Reflections from the Field. *International Journal of Educational Development,* 31(3), 185-192. https://doi.org/10.1016/j.ijedudev.2010.06.009
28. Singh, P. (2017). The Social and Economic Impacts of Child Labour in Rural India. *Indian Journal of Social Issues,* 8(4), 125-137.
29. Skutnabb-Kangas, T., & Heugh, K. (Eds.). (2012). *Multilingual Education and Sustainable Diversity Work: From Periphery to Center.* Routledge.
30. Sriprakash, A. (2012). *Pedagogies for Development: The Politics and Practice of Child-centred Education in India.* Springer. https://doi.org/10.1057/9781137032759
31. UNESCO. (2010). *Reaching the Marginalized: EFA Global Monitoring Report 2010.* United Nations Educational, Scientific and Cultural Organization. https://unesdoc.unesco.org
32. UNESCO. (2017). *A Guide for Ensuring Inclusion and Equity in Education.* United Nations Educational, Scientific and Cultural Organization. https://unesdoc.unesco.org
33. UNICEF. (2019). *Child Abuse and Neglect: The Global State of Children.* https://www.unicef.org/reports/child-abuse
34. UNICEF. (2019). *Inclusive Education: Ensuring Access to Education for Every Child.* https://www.unicef.org

35. UNICEF India. (2019). *Including All Children in Education: Education for Social Inclusion*. https://www.unicef.org/india
36. UNODC. (2018). *The Impact of Child Soldiering in War Zones*. United Nations Office on Drugs and Crime. https://www.unodc.org/child-soldiers.
37. Vedavalli, S. (2015). Multigrade Teaching in Indian Primary Schools: A Neglected Model for Quality Education. *International Journal of Educational Development*, 43, 63-72. https://doi.org/10.1016/j.ijedudev.2015.04.005
38. World Bank. (2017). *Inclusion and Education: All means all*. https://www.worldbank.org

4 CHAPTER

Constitutional Provisions and Recommendations

INTRODUCTION

The Indian Constitution provides a robust framework for the empowerment of marginalized communities, ensuring social justice, equality, and inclusive development. It enshrines the rights of Scheduled Castes (SCs), Scheduled Tribes (STs), Other Backward Classes (OBCs), women, and persons with disabilities through various Articles, including Article 15 (prohibition of discrimination), Article 17 (abolition of untouchability), Article 46 (promotion of educational and economic interests of SCs, STs and other weaker sections), and Article 16 (equal opportunity in public employment). These provisions aim to correct historical injustices and promote equitable participation in the nation's progress. Over the decades, numerous commissions and committees have provided significant policy recommendations to enhance the status of marginalized groups. The Mandal Commission report of 1980 played a transformative role by recommending reservations in government jobs and educational institutions for OBCs, recognizing the need for affirmative action. Similarly, the Protection of Civil Rights Act (1976) and the Prevention of Atrocities Act (1989) were landmark legal instruments that aimed to curb social discrimination and violence against SCs and STs.

The National Commission for SCs and STs (2000) was constituted to monitor and safeguard the rights and interests of these communities. The commission's reports have informed legislative and administrative actions aimed at enhancing access to education, employment, and social welfare. Furthermore, the Kothari Commission (1964-66) emphasized equality of educational opportunity and advocated for common schooling as a means to bridge social divides.The National Policy on Education (1986), followed by its Programme of Action (1992), laid a strong emphasis on inclusive education and highlighted the need to provide free and compulsory education to all children, especially from disadvantaged backgrounds. It emphasized compensatory measures, scholarships, special hostels, and remedial coaching to bridge the learning gap for SC/ST and other marginalized learners. The National Curriculum Framework (2005) called for a learner-centred approach and encouraged curricular reforms that addressed the diversity in learners' backgrounds. It advocated for inclusive pedagogy and content that reflected the pluralistic nature of Indian society. This framework stressed the need to remove biases in textbooks and create culturally responsive learning environments.

The Sachar Committee Report (2006) drew national attention to the socio-economic and educational status of Muslims in India. It highlighted their underrepresentation in educational institutions and public employment and led to targeted interventions and scholarship programs to address these gaps. It also called for the improvement of minority educational institutions and greater access to skill development opportunities. The New Education Policy (NEP) 2020 envisions an Inclusive and equitable education system by 2040, with special emphasis on disadvantaged groups. It proposes a holistic framework to ensure universal access to quality education and focuses on early childhood care, foundational literacy, and the integration of vocational education. The NEP also stresses the need to bring dropouts back into the education system and foster multilingualism to overcome linguistic barriers.

Educational provisions have been specially designed for SCs, STs, OBCs, OECs, women, and other marginalized sections. Scholarships, residential schools, mid-day meal schemes, and bridge courses are part of the broader effort to ensure retention and successful learning outcomes. Institutions like Navodaya Vidyalayas and Kasturba Gandhi Balika Vidyalayas also cater to the educational needs of these groups. The Persons with Disabilities Act (PWD) of 1995 and its subsequent revision in 2016 (Rights of Persons with Disabilities Act) strengthened the legal mandate for inclusive education, accessibility, and non-discrimination in educational institutions and workplaces. It expanded the categories of disabilities recognized and emphasized inclusive pedagogy and reasonable accommodations in schools and colleges. Reservations in education and public employment have played a critical role in ensuring that marginalized groups gain access to opportunities traditionally denied to them. These policies, coupled with vocational training initiatives and financial assistance programs, aim to create an equitable society where everyone has the chance to achieve

CONSTITUTIONAL PROVISIONS FOR THE EMPOWERMENT OF MARGINALIZED GROUPS

The Constitution of India provides a comprehensive framework to uplift and empower marginalized communities, including Scheduled Castes (SCs), Scheduled Tribes (STs), Other Backward Classes (OBCs), religious minorities, women, and persons with disabilities. From the outset, the Preamble sets the tone by emphasizing justice, equality, and fraternity for all citizens. This foundational vision ensures that the Constitution actively promotes the inclusion of those historically oppressed and excluded from mainstream society.

Part III of the Constitution, which deals with Fundamental Rights, offers critical protections to marginalized groups. Article 14 guarantees equality before the law, and Article 15 prohibits discrimination based on religion, race, caste, sex, or place of birth. It also allows for affirmative action in favour of disadvantaged communities. Article 17 abolishes untouchability, making it a punishable offense, and stands as a powerful statement against caste-based discrimination. These rights are enforceable in a court of law and act as a legal shield for the vulnerable.

To guide state policy, the Directive Principles of State Policy in Part IV of the Constitution emphasize socio-economic justice. Article 46 specifically urges the state to promote the educational and economic interests of SCs, STs, and other weaker sections, protecting them from social injustice and exploitation. Although not legally enforceable, these principles have shaped various welfare programs and reservation policies aimed at bridging inequalities.

Political empowerment is another cornerstone of the Constitution's inclusive approach. Articles 330 and 332 provide for the reservation of seats for SCs and STs in the Parliament and State Legislative Assemblies. Further, the 73rd and 74th Amendments mandate reservation in Panchayati Raj Institutions and Urban Local Bodies, not only for SCs and STs but also for women, thus ensuring democratic representation at the grassroots level.

Constitutional bodies like the National Commission for Scheduled Castes (Article 338) and the National Commission for Scheduled Tribes (Article 338A) play a vital role in monitoring safeguards and recommending policy measures. These bodies provide institutional support to marginalized groups and act as watchdogs to ensure their rights are upheld. Together, these constitutional provisions work toward the vision of a just and equitable society, actively addressing historical disadvantages and creating opportunities for inclusive growth.The Indian Constitution has several provisions aimed at empowering marginalized groups, including:

- Provisions for Scheduled Castes (SCs) and Scheduled Tribes (STs)
- **Reservation of Seats:** Reservation of seats in the Lok Sabha and State Legislative Assemblies for SCs and STs (Articles 330 and 332)
- **National Commission for Scheduled Castes (NCSC):** The NCSC investigates matters related to SCs and reports to the President (Article 338)
- **National Commission for Scheduled Tribes (NCST):** The NCST looks after the protection and development of STs (Article 338A)

Provisions for Women

- **Equality Before Law:** Article 14 ensures equality before the law for all citizens, including women
- **No Discrimination:** Article 15 prohibits discrimination on grounds of sex
- **Equal Opportunity:** Article 16 ensures equal opportunity for women in public employment
- **National Commission for Women (NCW):** The NCW works towards protecting and promoting women's rights

Provisions for Minorities

- **Protection of Interests:** Article 29 protects the interests of minorities
- **Right to Establish Educational Institutions:** Article 30 allows minorities to establish educational institutions
- **National Commission for Minorities (NCM):** The NCM works towards protecting and promoting minority rights

Provisions for Backward Classes

- **National Commission for Backward Classes (NCBC):** The NCBC examines requests for inclusion in the list of backward classes
- **Reservation:** Reservation of seats in public employment and educational institutions for backward classes [Article 16(4)]

Other Provisions

- **Directive Principles of State Policy:** Articles 38, 39, and 46 direct the state to promote social and economic justice for marginalized groups
- **Special Provisions:** Articles 371 to 371J provide special provisions for certain states and regions

These provisions aim to promote social and economic equality and provide opportunities for marginalized groups to participate in the country's development.

RECOMMENDATIONS OF VARIOUS COMMISSIONS AND POLICIES

The Mandal Commission Report (1980), officially known as the Second Backward Classes Commission, was a landmark in recognizing the need for affirmative action for Other Backward Classes (OBCs). Headed by B.P. Mandal, the commission identified socially and educationally backward classes and recommended 27% reservation in government jobs and educational institutions. This brought the total reservation to 49.5%, sparking national debate but ultimately strengthening the legal framework for positive discrimination.

The Protection of Civil Rights Act (1976) was enacted to give effect to Article 17 of the Constitution, which abolishes untouchability. The Act prescribes punishments for preventing a person from using public spaces, services, and institutions due to caste-based discrimination. It reinforced the idea that social dignity must be safeguarded for all, especially the Scheduled Castes, and provided the legal means to combat caste-based exclusions.

The Prevention of Atrocities Act (1989) was a further step to protect SCs and STs from targeted violence and systemic discrimination. The Act lists specific offenses, including social boycotts, physical violence, and destruction of property, and prescribes stringent punishments. It also established Special Courts and public prosecutors to handle such cases efficiently, thereby offering marginalized communities' legal recourse against caste-based atrocities.

The National Commission for Scheduled Castes and Scheduled Tribes (2000) was established under Articles 338 and 338A of the Constitution. This constitutional body monitors the implementation of safeguards and reviews policies related to the welfare of SCs and STs. The Commission submits annual reports to the President, making critical recommendations regarding discrimination, access to justice, and socio-economic development.

The Kothari Commission Report (1964-66), officially the Education Commission, emphasized the role of education in achieving social justice. It recommended a common school system and stressed the importance of inclusive education for national integration. It also advocated for equal educational opportunities regardless of caste, gender, or economic status, laying the foundation for many future policies.

The National Policy on Education (1986) reinforced the commitment to equity and access in education. It proposed Operation Blackboard to improve infrastructure, and the District Primary Education Programme (DPEP) to universalize elementary education. The policy emphasized removing disparities, especially among disadvantaged groups like girls, SCs, STs, and minorities, thus promoting inclusive development.

The Programme of Action (1992) was formulated to implement the NPE 1986 more effectively. It prioritized free and compulsory education for all children up to the age of 14 and called for curriculum revision to reflect national values, scientific temper, and social justice. Special focus was placed on enhancing the enrolment and retention of marginalized children, particularly those from SC/ST backgrounds.

The National Curriculum Framework (2005) further developed the idea of inclusive education. It proposed child-centred pedagogy, recognition of diversity in classrooms, and gender sensitivity. It also called for textbooks to be free from stereotypes and encouraged curriculum reform that respects linguistic, cultural, and social pluralism, thereby addressing systemic biases in the educational system.

The Sachar Committee Report (2006) was a pivotal document assessing the socio-economic and educational status of Muslims in India. It revealed that Muslims were among the most educationally and economically disadvantaged groups and recommended targeted interventions in education, employment, and access to public services. The report spurred policy debates on minority welfare and inclusive governance.

Finally, the Vision of the National Education Policy (2020) is transformative in its outlook. It focuses on equity and inclusion, especially for historically marginalized and disadvantaged groups. The NEP 2020 envisions a flexible curriculum, mother-tongue instruction, and better integration of vocational education. It underscores the need to bring dropouts back into school and bridge learning gaps for SCs, STs, OBCs, minorities, and differently-abled learners.

MANDAL COMMISSION REPORT

The Mandal Commission, officially known as the Second Backward Classes Commission, was established in 1979 under the chairmanship of B.P. Mandal by the Government of India. The primary aim was to identify the socially and educationally backward classes in India and recommend measures for their advancement.

The Commission submitted its report in 1980, identifying Other Backward Classes (OBCs) as comprising approximately 52% of India's population. It recommended a 27% reservation in government jobs and educational institutions for OBCs, in addition to the existing 22.5% reservation for Scheduled Castes and Scheduled Tribes. This would bring the total reservation to 49.5%, a landmark in India's affirmative action framework. The report emphasized that economic development alone could not eradicate social backwardness without addressing deep-rooted caste-based discrimination.

Despite significant political resistance and protests, especially after the implementation of the report in the 1990s, the Mandal Commission fundamentally reshaped India's approach to social justice. It laid the groundwork for positive discrimination policies, giving historically marginalized communities greater access to employment, education, and political representation.

PROTECTION OF CIVIL RIGHTS ACT (1976)

The Protection of Civil Rights Act, originally enacted in 1955 and amended in 1976, was a legislative step to enforce Article 17 of the Indian Constitution, which abolishes untouchability in all forms. The Act criminalizes any form of discrimination based on untouchability and aims to provide equal access to public spaces, institutions, and services for individuals belonging to Scheduled Castes (SCs) and other marginalized groups.

Under the 1976 amendment, the Act was strengthened by increasing penalties for offenses and expanding its scope. It prohibits denying entry to places of worship, access to public facilities (like shops, restaurants, and schools), and the use of public wells, roads, or transport. The law also addresses the refusal to sell goods or render services to individuals due to caste-based prejudice. Special provisions were made for speedy trial of offenses under this Act. Despite its progressive intent, challenges in implementation due to social resistance, inadequate awareness, and underreporting have persisted. However, the Act remains a cornerstone in India's legal efforts to protect marginalized groups and promote social equity and justice.

THE SCHEDULED CASTES AND THE SCHEDULED TRIBES (PREVENTION OF ATROCITIES) ACT, 1989

The Prevention of Atrocities (PoA) Act, 1989 was enacted to address the persistent and severe forms of violence, discrimination, and exploitation faced by members of the Scheduled Castes (SCs) and Scheduled Tribes (STs). While the Indian Constitution provides legal safeguards, the PoA Act was introduced to give these protections stronger enforcement and to deter crimes against these marginalized communities.

The Act defines a wide range of atrocities such as physical assault, sexual violence, forced labour, social boycotts, denial of access to public resources, and destruction of property. It mandates stringent punishments for perpetrators and introduces Special Courts and Exclusive Public Prosecutors for the speedy trial of offenses. The Act also includes provisions for relief and rehabilitation of victims and holds public servants accountable for neglect of duty in preventing such offenses.

Despite implementation challenges, including delays in prosecution and underreporting, the Act remains a critical legal instrument in protecting the dignity, rights, and lives of SCs and STs. Amendments over the years, including in 2015 and 2018, have further strengthened the law by expanding definitions and removing procedural hurdles.

NATIONAL COMMISSION FOR SCHEDULED CASTES AND SCHEDULED TRIBES – 2000 REPORT

The National Commission for Scheduled Castes and Scheduled Tribes (SC/ST), established under Article 338 of the Indian Constitution, functions as a watchdog for the protection and advancement of SC/ST rights. The 2000 report highlighted systemic challenges, the persistent practice of untouchability, socio-economic marginalization, and lapses in the implementation of welfare schemes meant for SC/ST communities.

Key recommendations of the 2000 report included effective enforcement of reservation policies in public employment, education, and political representation. It urged for better allocation and timely release of funds under SC/ST development programs and stressed the need for monitoring mechanisms at the central and state levels to evaluate policy outcomes. The Commission also emphasized land redistribution, skill development, and access to quality education as pivotal tools for empowerment.

Another significant aspect was the recommendation to strengthen grievance redressal mechanisms, including fast-tracking of cases under the Prevention of Atrocities Act and ensuring accountability of public officials in cases of negligence or discrimination. The report called for greater community participation and awareness campaigns to dismantle the social stigmas still prevalent in many parts of India.

KOTHARI COMMISSION REPORT (1964-66)

The Kothari Commission, officially known as the Education Commission (1964-66), was appointed by the Government of India under the chairmanship of Dr. D.S. Kothari, to examine the entire educational system and recommend reforms to make education more effective, inclusive, and equitable. The Commission's report was a landmark in shaping modern Indian education policy, with a strong emphasis on social justice and national integration.

The Commission stressed the need for a common school system to reduce disparities between different socio-economic groups and ensure that education becomes a tool for social mobility. It recommended free and compulsory education for children up to the age of 14, and special incentives for children from marginalized communities, including Scheduled Castes,

Scheduled Tribes, and girls. The report also highlighted the need for vocational education, teacher training, and curriculum reform to make education relevant to national development.

One of its most influential ideas was the 10+2+3 structure of education, which later became the national pattern. The Commission's vision helped lay the groundwork for subsequent policies aimed at bridging educational gaps, promoting equality of opportunity, and addressing the specific needs of disadvantaged sections of society.

NATIONAL POLICY ON EDUCATION (1986)

The National Policy on Education (NPE) 1986 was a pivotal reform initiative by the Government of India aimed at addressing the disparities and challenges in the Indian education system. It emphasized the role of education as a powerful instrument for reducing inequality, promoting social justice, and empowering marginalized communities, particularly Scheduled Castes (SCs), Scheduled Tribes (STs), women, and other disadvantaged groups.

One of the major recommendations of the policy was to improve access and retention of students from marginalized sections through non-formal education, bridge courses, and support services like scholarships, free textbooks, and hostels. The policy also emphasized the development of educational infrastructure in rural and tribal areas and called for the strengthening of primary education as the foundation of national development. It proposed the establishment of Navodaya Vidyalayas to provide quality education to talented children from rural areas.

Additionally, the NPE (1986) highlighted the importance of curriculum reform to reflect the constitutional values of secularism, equality, and national integration, and the need to eliminate gender bias and caste discrimination in textbooks and teaching practices. It also advocated for teacher training and community involvement to create an inclusive learning environment.

PROGRAMME OF ACTION (1992)

The Programme of Action (POA), 1992 was developed as a follow-up to the National Policy on Education (NPE), 1986 to provide a concrete implementation framework for the policy's goals and recommendations. It aimed to translate the policy's broad objectives into actionable strategies with a special emphasis on equity, access, and quality education for marginalized groups, including Scheduled Castes (SCs), Scheduled Tribes (STs), girls, and minorities.

A core aspect of the POA was its commitment to Universalisation of Elementary Education (UEE). It proposed the expansion of schooling facilities, especially in underserved rural and tribal areas, and promoted the use of alternative schooling methods such as non-formal education centres and bridge courses. To tackle dropout rates among marginalized children, the POA recommended mid-day meal schemes, incentives, and remedial teaching.

The POA also addressed Issues of curriculum development, calling for content that is inclusive, culturally sensitive, and free from gender and caste bias. It emphasized teacher education and training, particularly for those serving in disadvantaged regions, and proposed greater community involvement in managing and monitoring schools. Overall, the POA served as a detailed roadmap to realize the egalitarian and inclusive vision of NPE 1986, focusing on empowering the most vulnerable groups through targeted educational interventions.

NATIONAL CURRICULUM FRAMEWORK (2005)

The National Curriculum Framework (NCF) 2005, developed by the National Council of Educational Research and Training (NCERT), was a key educational reform document aimed at shaping teaching and learning in a way that promotes equity, inclusion, and quality. Building on earlier policy frameworks, including the National Policy on Education (1986) and the Programme of Action (1992), the NCF focused on making education more child-centred and relevant to India's diverse socio-cultural context.

One of the framework's central themes was inclusion of marginalized groups, such as Scheduled Castes (SCs), Scheduled Tribes (STs), minorities, children with disabilities, and those in remote and disadvantaged areas. The NCF advocated for contextual and flexible curricula that reflect local knowledge, languages, and cultural practices. It also emphasized eliminating caste, gender, and religious biases from textbooks and teaching practices.

The framework promoted constructivist learning, encouraging students to actively construct knowledge through interaction with their environment rather than rote learning. It called for multilingualism, encouraging the use of mother tongues as the medium of instruction at the primary level and promoting respect for linguistic diversity. Teachers were envisioned as facilitators and guides, requiring ongoing professional development and community support.By emphasizing the principles of democracy, secularism, equality, and social justice, the NCF 2005 laid a foundation for an inclusive education system that addresses the learning needs of all children, particularly the marginalized and underrepresented.

SACHAR COMMITTEE REPORT (2006)

The Sachar Committee, formally known as the Prime Minister's High-Level Committee on the Social, Economic and Educational Status of the

Muslim Community of India, was constituted in 2005 and chaired by Justice Rajinder Sachar. Its 2006 report was a landmark document that provided a data-driven analysis of the conditions of Muslims in India and offered significant recommendations for their inclusion and development.

The committee found that Indian Muslims were lagging behind other communities in almost all socio-economic indicators, including education, employment, income, housing, and access to public services. It highlighted underrepresentation in public institutions and a perception of alienation and marginalization among Muslim citizens. One of its key recommendations was the establishment of an Equal Opportunity Commission to ensure non-discriminatory access to education, employment, and housing.

In education, the report advocated for improving access to quality schooling in Muslim-dominated areas, enhancing scholarships, and upgrading infrastructure in madrasas through modernization schemes. It also called for better representation of Muslims in government jobs, creation of Muslim-majority development blocks, and inclusion in government welfare schemes like Sarva Shiksha Abhiyan and Integrated Child Development Services (ICDS).The Sachar Report underscored the urgent need for inclusive development policies, institutional reforms, and a shift in perception to ensure that Muslims, as a significant minority group, are treated as equal citizens and active contributors to India's socio-economic growth.

NATIONAL EDUCATION POLICY (NEP) 2020

The National Education Policy (NEP) 2020, approved by the Government of India, represents a comprehensive overhaul of the Indian education system with a vision to make it more inclusive, accessible, and equitable. The policy aims to provide quality education to all children, with a special focus on marginalized communities, Scheduled Castes (SCs), Scheduled Tribes (STs), women, and linguistic minorities. It is designed to create a system that fosters critical thinking, creativity, and holistic development while bridging disparities in education.

Key recommendations include the integration of education with local contexts, particularly through the use of mother tongues in early education. The policy stresses multilingualism, encouraging the learning of multiple languages to ensure inclusivity and broader access. It also calls for the establishment of model schools in rural and underserved areas to serve as centres of excellence. One of its significant initiatives is the increased focus on vocational education and skill-building, ensuring that marginalized children have pathways to employable skills.

The NEP 2020 advocates for a rigorous, community-based monitoring system to ensure that marginalized groups are not left behind, and their specific needs are addressed. In addition, it recommends the expansion of scholarships, financial support, and special educational provisions for children from vulnerable sections. The policy envisions the promotion of digital literacy, especially in rural areas, and the introduction of flexible learning paths to cater to children with different learning needs. Through the inclusion of marginalized communities in all levels of education, the NEP 2020 envisions a system where every child, regardless of their socio-economic status or background, has an equal opportunity to learn, grow, and succeed.

EDUCATIONAL PROVISIONS FOR SC/ST, OBC, OEC, WOMEN, AND OTHER BACKWARD CLASSES

The Indian Constitution and subsequent government policies have laid a strong foundation for ensuring educational equity for marginalized and disadvantaged communities such as Scheduled Castes (SCs), Scheduled Tribes (STs), Other Backward Classes (OBCs), Other Economically Backward Classes (OECs), and women. The primary objective has been to bridge the historical gap in access, retention, and quality of education for these groups through affirmative action, special schemes, and financial support mechanisms.

For SC and ST communities, various central and state governments have implemented reservation policies in educational institutions, extending to central universities, IITs, and public schools. The Post-Matric Scholarship Scheme, Pre-Matric Scholarships, hostel facilities, and remedial coaching centres are major support systems. Institutions like Navodaya Vidyalayas and Kendriya Vidyalayas also aim to provide quality education for students from marginalized backgrounds. The Right to Education Act (2009) also mandates free and compulsory education for all children aged 6-14, indirectly benefiting SC/ST children.

OBCs are also entitled to 27% reservation in higher education institutions. Scholarships and financial assistance programs like the National Fellowship for OBC Students and skill development initiatives have been established to increase their participation in technical and professional education. Special coaching programs for competitive exams and entrance tests are also provided to enhance representation and success rates among OBC youth.Other Economically Backward Classes (OECs), particularly recognized in some Indian states like Kerala, receive support similar to OBCs through targeted scholarships, fee concessions, and hostel allowances. Though the central government has not always had separate schemes for OECs, state governments often ensure their inclusion through localized educational and welfare policies.

Women from marginalized communities face compounded disadvantages due to both gender and social status. To address this, schemes such as Beti Bachao, Beti Padhao, Kasturba Gandhi Balika Vidyalaya, and Girls' Hostel schemes focus on increasing enrolment, reducing dropouts, and improving infrastructure for girls. Reservation in universities, financial incentives for parents, and vocational training centres for adolescent girls contribute to bridging the gender gap in education, particularly in rural and tribal areas. Overall, the government continues to focus on inclusive education by adopting policies and strategies that not only promote access and retention but also quality and relevance of education for marginalized groups. Continued efforts are essential to reduce disparities, enhance digital and language inclusion, and ensure that no group is left behind in India's educational landscape.

EDUCATIONAL PROVISIONS FOR SC/ST, OBC, OEC, WOMEN, AND OTHER BACKWARD CLASSES

Constitutional Provisions

- **Article 15(4):** Empowers the state to make special provisions for the advancement of socially and educationally backward classes, including SCs and STs, regarding admissions to educational institutions.
- **Article 15(5):** Allows the state to establish special arrangements for backward classes, SCs, or STs for admission to private educational institutions.
- **Article 16(4):** Enables the state to reserve positions in the public sector for backward classes underrepresented in the public sector.
- **Article 46:** Directs the state to promote educational and economic interests of SCs, STs, and weaker sections.

Provisions for SC/ST

- **Reservation:** Seats are reserved for SCs and STs in educational institutions and government jobs.
- **Scholarships:** Various scholarships are available for SC/ST students to pursue higher education.
- **Special Schemes:** Initiatives like Sarva Shiksha Abhiyan (SSA), Mid-Day Meal Scheme, and Kasturba Gandhi Balika Vidyalayas aim to improve education and welfare of SC/ST students.

Provisions for OBC

- **Reservation:** OBCs are eligible for reservations in educational institutions and government jobs.

- **National Commission for Backward Classes (NCBC):** Advises the government on inclusion and exclusion of communities in the OBC category.
- **Scholarships and Skill Development:** Various programs are available to support OBC students and youth.

Provisions for Women

- **Equal Opportunity:** Women have equal rights to education and employment.
- **Special Schemes:** Initiatives like Beti Bachao Beti Padhao and schemes for girls' education aim to promote women's education and empowerment.
- **Scholarships and Financial Support:** Various scholarships and financial support programs are available for women students.

Provisions for Other Backward Classes (OEC): Similar to OBCs, OECs may be eligible for reservations and benefits, depending on their specific categorization and government policies.

Key Initiatives

- **Sarva Shiksha Abhiyan (SSA):** Aims to universalize elementary education.
- **Mid-Day Meal Scheme:** Provides meals to students in government schools.
- **National Institute of Open Schooling (NIOS):** Offers open schooling options for students.
- **Kendriya Vidyalayas (KVS):** Provides quality education to children of central government employees.

PERSONS WITH DISABILITIES (PWD) ACT 1995 AND THE RIGHTS OF PERSONS WITH DISABILITIES (RPWD) ACT 2016

The Persons with Disabilities (Equal Opportunities, Protection of Rights and Full Participation) Act, 1995 was India's first comprehensive law to safeguard the rights and dignity of individuals with disabilities. Enacted in response to the UN General Assembly's 1992 proclamation on equal opportunities for persons with disabilities, the Act recognized seven categories of disabilities and aimed to ensure full participation and equality. It mandated equal access to education, employment, and infrastructure, while also providing for 3% reservation in government jobs and educational institutions.

While progressive for its time, the 1995 Act was found lacking after India ratified the UN Convention on the Rights of Persons with Disabilities

(UNCRPD) in 2007. To bridge these gaps, the government enacted the Rights of Persons with Disabilities (RPwD) Act, 2016, which came into effect in 2017. This Act expanded the recognized disabilities from 7 to 21, including conditions such as autism, cerebral palsy, thalassemia, multiple sclerosis, and specific learning disabilities, thus broadening the scope of protection and inclusion.

The RPwD Act of 2016 introduced stronger enforcement mechanisms and legal remedies. It increased the reservation in government jobs from 3% to 4% and in higher education from 3% to 5%. The Act mandated inclusive education and barrier-free access in all public spaces. Importantly, it emphasized non-discrimination, equal legal rights, and full participation of persons with disabilities in political and social life. Guardianship rights, social security, and the right to equal protection under the law were also addressed more comprehensively. This legislative transition from the PWD Act of 1995 to the RPwD Act of 2016 reflects India's evolving commitment to social justice and human rights for persons with disabilities. The newer law ensures alignment with international norms and provides a more holistic approach to empower persons with disabilities, promoting dignity, independence, and equality in all spheres of life.

- Persons with Disabilities (Equal Opportunities, Protection of Rights and Full Participation) Act, 1995
- The PWD Act, 1995 was India's first major legislation aimed at promoting the rights of persons with disabilities. It was enacted to fulfill India's obligations under the UN Convention on the Rights of Persons with Disabilities (UNCRPD).

Key features:

- Recognized seven disabilities including blindness, low vision, leprosy-cured, hearing impairment, locomotor disability, mental retardation, and mental illness.
- Focused on equal opportunities in education, employment, and access to public facilities.
- Provided reservation of 3% in government jobs and educational institutions.
- Ensured barrier-free access to buildings and transport.
- Emphasized the integration and mainstreaming of persons with disabilities into society.

However, the 1995 Act was limited in scope and did not fully align with the UNCRPD, leading to the formulation of a more comprehensive law in 2016.

Rights of Persons with Disabilities (RPwD) Act, 2016: Replacing the 1995 Act, the RPwD Act, 2016 came into force to provide stronger protection and enforcement of the rights of persons with disabilities. It aligns with international standards and India's commitment under the UNCRPD.

Key features:

- Expanded the list to 21 types of disabilities, including autism, cerebral palsy, multiple sclerosis, thalassemia, and speech and language disability.
- Increased reservation in government jobs from 3% to 4% and in higher education from 3% to 5%.
- Emphasized non-discrimination, equal protection under the law, and reasonable accommodation.
- Mandated the creation of inclusive education systems and barrier-free environments.
- Introduced provisions for guardianship, legal capacity, and penalties for discrimination.
- Called for the formation of Central and State Advisory Boards to monitor implementation.

RESERVATION AND OPPORTUNITIES FOR EDUCATION AND VOCATION

India's constitutional and legal framework provides affirmative action policies to promote educational and vocational opportunities for historically marginalized communities, including Scheduled Castes (SC), Scheduled Tribes (ST), Other Backward Classes (OBC), Persons with Disabilities (PwDs), and economically weaker sections. One of the key tools for ensuring inclusivity has been the system of reservations in education and public employment. These provisions are aimed at correcting historical injustices and ensuring equal access to resources and opportunities.

In the education sector, reservations are provided in public educational institutions including central universities, IITs, IIMs, and other higher education institutes. Typically, 15% of seats are reserved for SCs, 7.5% for STs, 27% for OBCs, and 10% for Economically Weaker Sections (EWS) under the 103rd Constitutional Amendment Act. For Persons with Disabilities, a reservation of 5% in higher education is mandated under the Rights of Persons with Disabilities Act, 2016. Alongside reservation, various scholarship schemes (like Post-Matric Scholarships, National Fellowship for SC/ST students, and UGC-NET JRFs) and coaching assistance programs are implemented to support students' academic success.

In terms of vocational opportunities, the Indian government has initiated several programs such as the Skill India Mission, Deen Dayal

Upadhyaya Grameen Kaushalya Yojana (DDU-GKY), and Pradhan Mantri Kaushal Vikas Yojana (PMKVY). These focus on providing skill development training, vocational education, and employment linkages, especially for rural youth, women, and members of SC/ST/OBC communities. Special vocational training centers also operate for persons with disabilities under the National Handicapped Finance and Development Corporation (NHFDC).

These initiatives aim to ensure that marginalized groups are not only included in the mainstream of society but are also empowered to contribute actively through education and employment. The combination of reservations, financial aid, skill training, and policy support reflects a comprehensive approach to equitable development in India.Reservation policies in India aim to promote social justice and equality by providing opportunities for historically marginalized communities in education and employment. Here's a breakdown of the benefits and challenges:

Education Benefits

- Increased representation of Scheduled Castes (SCs) and Scheduled Tribes (STs) in higher education institutions
- Improved access to education for underprivileged sections of society
- Reservation policies have led to a marked increase in enrolment rates among SCs and STs

Employment Benefits

- Reservation policies ensure adequate representation of marginalized communities in public sector jobs
- Increased diversity in government positions and departments
- 4% reservation for people with disabilities in government jobs

Types of Reservations

- **Vertical Reservation:** For SCs, STs, and Other Backward Classes (OBCs) in education and employment
- **Horizontal Reservation:** For specific categories within reserved categories, such as differently-abled individuals
- **Caste-Based Reservation:** For historically marginalized castes
- **Income-Based Reservation:** For economically weaker sections, such as the 10% reservation for Economically Weaker Sections (EWS)
- **Gender-Based Reservation:** One-third reservation for women in local bodies

Challenges

- **Creamy Layer:** Economically advanced individuals within reserved categories benefiting disproportionately
- **Social Stigma:** Individuals from reserved categories facing stigma or discrimination
- **Meritocracy vs. Equality:** Debate surrounding reservation policies and their impact on meritocracy
- **Corruption and Instrumentalization:** Challenges in implementing reservation policies, including corruption in caste certification and political instrumentalization

Reforms

- Integrating economic criteria into reservation policies
- Expanding skill development programs
- Enforcing anti-discrimination laws in private employment

Overall, reservation policies have transformed the landscape of education and employment in India, promoting socio-economic mobility for millions. However, challenges persist, and ongoing debates highlight the need for adaptive policies that address evolving inequalities.

CONCLUSION

The empowerment of marginalized groups in India remains a constitutional and moral imperative that continues to evolve in both scope and implementation. The Constitution of India lays a strong foundation through provisions that guarantee equality, prohibit discrimination, and ensure affirmative action in favour of the socially and educationally disadvantaged. These constitutional safeguards have been pivotal in initiating a journey toward inclusive and equitable development.The efforts to empower marginalized communities have been reinforced by various landmark commissions and policy documents. The Mandal Commission catalysed a shift in public policy by advocating for the inclusion of OBCs in reservation frameworks. Similarly, the Protection of Civil Rights Act and the Prevention of Atrocities Act were crucial in legally recognizing and addressing the systemic oppression faced by SCs and STs, further strengthening legal accountability.

The National Commission for SCs and STs (2000) has functioned as a watchful authority to monitor policy implementation and redress grievances. Alongside, the Kothari Commission played an early yet important role in setting the tone for equality in education, advocating for a common school system and universal access as means to bridge social inequities. Education has been a powerful tool for empowerment, and national policies like the

NPE 1986 and its POA 1992 focused on reducing disparities through special programs, scholarships, and inclusive strategies. The National Curriculum Framework (2005) introduced curricular reforms to promote respect for diversity and discouraged caste, gender, and class biases within educational content and practice. The Sachar Committee Report brought minority concerns, particularly of the Muslim community, into sharper policy focus. By highlighting educational and socio-economic disadvantages, it emphasized the need for targeted interventions and institutional support for minority groups, including more inclusive schooling, better representation, and skill development initiatives.Vision NEP 2020 further expands the framework of inclusive education by calling for universal access, multilingual instruction, and curricular flexibility that caters to children from different backgrounds, particularly those who have been historically excluded. The policy envisions reducing dropout rates, improving foundational literacy, and creating equitable opportunities through the integration of vocational and academic learning.

Special educational provisions and schemes for SCs, STs, OBCs, OECs, women, and other marginalized groups have become more structured over the years. These include pre- and post-matric scholarships, free uniforms and books, residential schooling, and mid-day meals, all aimed at reducing barriers to education and increasing enrolment and retention. The PWD Acts of 1995 and 2016 have provided a comprehensive rights-based approach for persons with disabilities, ensuring their access to inclusive education, infrastructure accommodations, and participation in all spheres of life. These laws have widened the definition of disability and emphasized dignity, equity, and integration in education and employment. Reservation policies have not only enabled access to educational institutions and government employment for marginalized communities but have also initiated a cultural shift toward recognizing systemic exclusion. Along with vocational training programs and skill-building initiatives, these measures contribute to the economic independence and social mobility of disadvantaged groups.

In conclusion, while constitutional and legal measures have made significant strides in empowering marginalized communities, continued vigilance, implementation, and innovation are needed. Education remains central to this mission, serving as both a right and a catalyst for change. The progress achieved so far must be built upon through inclusive policies, social awareness, and sustained political will to create a truly equitable society.

KEY POINTS

- **Constitutional Provisions for Marginalized Groups:** The Indian Constitution provides a strong framework for the protection and empowerment of marginalized groups through Articles promoting equality, prohibiting discrimination, and enabling affirmative action in education and employment.

- **Mandal Commission Report:** The Mandal Commission (1980) identified socially and educationally backward classes and recommended 27% reservation for OBCs in public sector jobs and educational institutions to ensure equitable representation.
- **Protection of Civil Rights Act (1976):** This Act aims to eliminate untouchability and penalize caste-based discrimination, reinforcing the constitutional mandate of equality and social justice for marginalized communities.
- **Prevention of Atrocities Act (1989):** Designed to prevent violence and exploitation against Scheduled Castes and Scheduled Tribes, this Act strengthens legal protections and ensures accountability for caste-based atrocities.
- **National Commission for SC/ST (2000):** This commission monitors safeguards provided to SCs and STs under the Constitution and suggests measures for their development and protection.
- **Kothari Commission & National Policy on Education (1986):** These recommended a common school system and equitable education policies. The 1986 policy and its 1992 Programme of Action laid the foundation for inclusive educational practices and schemes.
- **National Curriculum Framework (2005):** The NCF introduced child-centric and inclusive pedagogy, promoting respect for diversity, reducing textbook biases, and addressing the learning needs of marginalized children.
- **Sachar Committee Report (2006):** This report examined the status of Muslims in India, highlighting disparities in education, employment, and governance, and called for remedial measures to promote equity.
- **Vision NEP 2020:** The National Education Policy 2020 focuses on inclusive, accessible, and equitable education for all, with particular attention to the needs of SCs, STs, OBCs, minorities, and persons with disabilities.
- **Educational Provisions and PWD Acts (1995 & 2016):** Special schemes provide scholarships, mid-day meals, free books, and hostels for SC/ST/OBC and girls. The PWD Acts guarantee inclusive education, skill development, and job opportunities for persons with disabilities.

REFERENCES

1. Austin, G. (1999). *Working a Democratic Constitution: The Indian Experience.* Oxford University Press.
2. Basu, D.D. (2013). *Introduction to the Constitution of India* (21st ed.). LexisNexis Butterworths.
3. Government of India. (1950). *The Constitution of India.* Ministry of Law and Justice. https://legislative.gov.in/constitution-of-india
4. Government of India. (1976). *The Protection of Civil Rights Act, 1955 (As Amended in 1976).* Ministry of Law and Justice.
5. Government of India. (1980). *Report of the Backward Classes Commission (Mandal Commission Report).* Ministry of Social Justice and Empowerment.
6. Government of India. (1986). *National Policy on Education, 1986.* Ministry of Education.
7. Government of India. (1989). *The Scheduled Castes and the Scheduled Tribes (Prevention of Atrocities) Act, 1989.* Ministry of Social Justice and Empowerment.
8. Government of India. (1992). *Programme of Action, 1992.* Ministry of Human Resource Development.
9. Government of India. (2009). *The Right of Children to Free and Compulsory Education Act, 2009.* Ministry of Law and Justice. https://legislative.gov.in
10. Government of India. (2016). *The Rights of Persons with Disabilities Act, 2016.* Ministry of Law and Justice. https://legislative.gov.in/sites/default/files/A2016-49_1.pdf
11. Government of India. (2019). *The Constitution (One Hundred and Third Amendment) Act, 2019.* Ministry of Law and Justice. https://legislative.gov.in
12. Kothari, D. S. (1966). *Report of the Education Commission, 1964-66.* Ministry of Education.
13. Ministry of Education. (2020). *National Education Policy 2020.* Government of India. https://www.education.gov.in/sites/upload_files/mhrd/files/NEP_Final_English_0.pdf
14. Ministry of Law and Justice. (1996). *The Persons with Disabilities (Equal Opportunities, Protection of Rights and Full Participation) Act, 1995.* Government of India. https://legislative.gov.in/sites/default/files/A1996-1.pdf
15. Ministry of Rural Development. (n.d.). *Deen Dayal Upadhyaya Grameen Kaushalya Yojana (DDU-GKY).* Government of India. https://ddugky.gov.in
16. Ministry of Skill Development and Entrepreneurship. (n.d.). *Pradhan Mantri Kaushal Vikas Yojana (PMKVY).* Government of India. https://www.pmkvyofficial.org
17. Ministry of Social Justice and Empowerment. (n.d.). *Post-Matric Scholarship for Scheduled Castes Students.* Government of India. https://socialjustice.gov.in
18. Ministry of Tribal Affairs. (n.d.). *Schemes for education of ST students.* Government of India. https://tribal.nic.in

19. Ministry of Women and Child Development. (n.d.). *Beti Bachao Beti Padhao Scheme*. Government of India. https://wcd.nic.in
20. National Commission for Backward Classes. (n.d.). *Functions and Activities*. Government of India. https://ncbc.nic.in
21. National Commission for Scheduled Castes and Scheduled Tribes. (2000). *Annual Reports*. Government of India.
22. National Council of Educational Research and Training (NCERT). (2005). *National Curriculum Framework 2005*. NCERT.
23. Pathak, A. (2002). Social Justice and the Constitution of India: An Analysis of Directive Principles. *Indian Journal of Public Administration*, 48(3), 379-390.
24. Sachar Committee. (2006). *Social, Economic and Educational Status of the Muslim Community of India*. Cabinet Secretariat.
25. Singh, M.P., & Saxena, R. (2011). *Indian Politics: Contemporary Issues and Concerns*. PHI Learning Pvt. Ltd.

5 CHAPTER

Empowering Marginalized Groups

INTRODUCTION

Women empowerment and social development have been central to the efforts of various national and international organizations. In recent years, agencies like UNDP, UNICEF, UNESCO, along with Non-Governmental Organizations (NGOs), Self-Help Groups (SHGs), Integrated Child Development Services (ICDS), and Early Childhood Care and Education (ECCE) have been playing vital roles in driving socio-economic transformation in rural and marginalized communities. These organizations and initiatives are not only aiming to improve access to education, healthcare, and livelihood but also striving to promote gender equality and ensure social justice for women and children. The United Nations Development Programme (UNDP) works extensively in promoting sustainable human development and reducing inequalities. Their interventions are aligned with national priorities and global Sustainable Development Goals (SDGs), focusing on improving the quality of life, supporting economic empowerment, and ensuring equal access to opportunities. Similarly, UNICEF's programs emphasize child protection, education, and nutrition, with a special focus on girls and marginalized groups. They work towards enhancing women's participation in decision-making processes and empowering children through access to education and health services.

The United Nations Educational, Scientific and Cultural Organization (UNESCO) also contributes to empowerment initiatives by focusing on education and knowledge-sharing. UNESCO's efforts in promoting gender equality, adult literacy programs, and women's involvement in leadership and governance are essential for creating a more inclusive and equitable society. Together, these international agencies provide resources, technical expertise, and advocacy to tackle global challenges faced by women and children. NGOs have been instrumental in implementing community-based projects that focus on capacity building, health, education, and economic development. These organizations often bridge gaps between local communities and government institutions, ensuring that the needs of women and children are addressed in a manner that is contextually relevant and culturally sensitive. Through their grassroots interventions, NGOs have contributed significantly to empowering women by facilitating access to resources, education, and healthcare.

Self-Help Groups (SHGs) are another key element in women empowerment, especially in rural areas. These groups, typically consisting of women from similar socio-economic backgrounds, work together to improve their social and financial status. By focusing on savings, credit, and income-generating activities, SHGs empower women to take control of their financial independence. Additionally, they provide a platform for women to discuss social issues, such as domestic violence, health, and legal rights, further promoting empowerment at the community level.ICDS and ECCE are government programs designed to improve the overall health, nutrition, and development of children, especially in underserved regions. ICDS provides a range of services, including supplementary nutrition, immunization, and preschool education. ECCE, as a part of the ICDS initiative, focuses on the early childhood years, laying the foundation for lifelong learning and development. These programs also play a pivotal role in encouraging maternal and child health, which directly impacts women's empowerment by enhancing their health and capacity to participate in the workforce.

In the context of women's empowerment, various government schemes such as Mahila Samakhya, Kishori Shakti Yojana, and the Rajiv Gandhi Scheme for Empowerment of Adolescent Girls are playing a transformative role. The Mahila Samakhya program focuses on strengthening women's collectives and providing them with the necessary skills and knowledge to engage in social and economic activities. The Kishori Shakti Yojana targets adolescent girls by improving their nutrition, health, and education, while the Rajiv Gandhi Scheme works towards empowering adolescent girls through skills development and educational support. These initiatives provide women and girls with the tools they need to thrive in both personal and professional spheres. Gram Panchayats, the local governing bodies at the village level, are crucial in promoting decentralized governance and enhancing community participation. Women's participation in these Panchayats has been encouraged through policies that reserve seats for women, ensuring their representation in local decision-making processes. This has not only empowered women but also helped address local challenges more effectively, especially in the domains of health, sanitation, education, and infrastructure. Community-based programs are another cornerstone of social development, focusing on enhancing the capabilities of local populations. These programs often integrate health, education, and economic support, directly engaging community members in decision-making and leadership. By empowering communities to address their own needs, these programs promote sustainable development and help uplift women and marginalized groups, particularly in rural and underserved areas.

Sustainable livelihood practices are essential for long-term empowerment. Through a combination of training in sustainable agricultural techniques, small-scale entrepreneurship, and access to microfinance, these practices help women build economic resilience and independence. Community-based sustainable livelihoods not only improve household income but also promote environmental sustainability, ensuring that future generations can benefit from a stable and healthy ecosystem. Lastly, minority scholarships offered by the government and NGOs play a crucial role in empowering women and children from minority communities. These scholarships provide financial support to pursue education and vocational training, ensuring that marginalized groups have equal access to opportunities for academic and professional growth. The scholarships serve as a tool for breaking the cycle of poverty and exclusion, fostering greater participation in the socio-economic mainstream. These efforts are key to achieving equitable development and creating a just society for all.

CONTRIBUTIONS OF DEVELOPMENT AGENCIES AND LOCAL INSTITUTIONS TO SOCIAL WELFARE AND EMPOWERMENT

The United Nations Development Programme (UNDP) plays a vital role in facilitating sustainable development by addressing poverty, inequality, and governance issues. It supports national and regional governments in policy formulation and implementation related to economic development, environmental sustainability, and inclusive growth. Through technical and financial assistance, UNDP strengthens institutions, promotes gender equality, and helps build resilience in communities.UNDP also engages with local bodies and communities to design and execute grassroots initiatives. Its work in digital empowerment, employment generation, and disaster risk reduction enables vulnerable populations to access resources and opportunities. By focusing on participatory governance and capacity building, UNDP contributes to long-term and inclusive development.

The United Nations Children's Fund (UNICEF) focuses on protecting and promoting the rights of children and women. It works across sectors like health, nutrition, education, water and sanitation, and child protection. UNICEF supports government programs such as immunization campaigns, mid-day meals, and early childhood education, aiming to improve child survival and development. In education, UNICEF collaborates with local stakeholders to ensure inclusive, equitable, and quality learning for all children. It develops child-friendly materials, trains teachers, and promotes safe learning environments. Its initiatives help reduce dropout rates, enhance learning outcomes, and ensure continuity of education during emergencies and crises.

The United Nations Educational, Scientific and Cultural Organization (UNESCO) plays a global role in fostering peace through education, science, and culture. It works to ensure universal access to quality education and promotes lifelong learning. In India, UNESCO supports literacy programs, heritage conservation, digital learning initiatives, and education for sustainable development.UNESCO's contributions in teacher training, curriculum development, and advocacy for inclusive education have had a significant impact. It promotes global citizenship, cultural diversity, and freedom of expression, which are essential for creating tolerant and knowledge-based societies.

Non-Governmental Organizations (NGOs) are instrumental in delivering services and advocating for rights in communities often neglected by mainstream systems. They work in fields such as education, health, environment, human rights, and rural development. NGOs collaborate with government bodies, international agencies, and communities to implement need-based projects.NGOs like Pratham, Akshaya Patra, and Help Age India have pioneered innovative solutions in literacy, mid-day meals, and elder care. Their grassroots presence and adaptability allow them to respond quickly to community needs and create lasting social impact through awareness, capacity building, and service delivery.

Self-Help Groups (SHGs) empower individuals, especially women, by providing a platform for savings, credit, and mutual support. These groups play a crucial role in promoting financial inclusion and economic independence at the community level. Through income-generating activities and collective bargaining, SHGs foster entrepreneurship and leadership. Government initiatives like the National Rural Livelihood Mission (NRLM) support SHGs by linking them to banks, markets, and skill training. SHGs often work in collaboration with Gram Panchayats and NGOs to ensure that women's voices are heard in local governance and development planning.

Integrated Child Development Services (ICDS) and Early Childhood Care and Education (ECCE) are central to the well-being and development of young children in India. ICDS provides a package of services, including nutrition, health check-ups, immunization, and early education through Anganwadi centres. ECCE focuses on the holistic development of children up to eight years, fostering their cognitive, emotional, and physical growth. Together, ICDS and ECCE ensure that children receive a strong start in life, especially those from disadvantaged backgrounds. With the integration of ECCE into the formal school system under the National Education Policy (NEP) 2020, these services are becoming more structured and accessible, contributing to improved learning outcomes and long-term societal progress.

Gram Panchayats, the basic units of local self-governance in rural India, are pivotal in implementing welfare schemes and ensuring community participation. They are responsible for local development plans, monitoring government programs, and delivering essential services like sanitation, drinking water, and education. Their proximity to the community enables them to address grassroots issues effectively. Gram Panchayats collaborate with SHGs, NGOs, ICDS centers, and health workers to provide integrated services. Their role in participatory planning and democratic decision-making empowers citizens and enhances accountability. By acting as a bridge between the government and the people, Gram Panchayats contribute significantly to inclusive rural development.

ROLE OF UNITED NATIONS DEVELOPMENT PROGRAMME (UNDP)

The United Nations Development Programme (UNDP) is the leading global development network of the United Nations. Its primary role is to help countries eliminate poverty, achieve sustainable development, and promote democratic governance. UNDP works in nearly 170 countries and territories, partnering with governments, civil society, and private organizations to design and implement development strategies that are inclusive, resilient, and environmentally sustainable. In India and other developing nations, UNDP supports programs focused on improving livelihoods, advancing gender equality, enhancing access to education and health services, and promoting clean energy and environmental protection. It provides technical assistance, policy advice, and funding for initiatives such as skill development for youth, digital governance, and climate adaptation projects. By strengthening institutions and fostering innovation, UNDP enables communities to build resilience against social, economic, and environmental challenges.

- **Poverty Reduction:** UNDP works to reduce poverty and inequality, promoting sustainable development.
- **Education and Skills:** UNDP supports initiatives that enhance education and skills development, particularly for marginalized communities.
- **Gender Equality:** UNDP promotes gender equality and empowers women and girls through various programs.

ROLE OF UNITED NATIONS CHILDREN'S FUND (UNICEF)

UNICEF is a global organization dedicated to protecting and promoting the rights and well-being of children and women. Its primary role is to ensure that every child has access to health care, education, nutrition, protection, and a safe environment. Working in over 190 countries, UNICEF partners with governments, NGOs, and communities to implement programs that support child survival, development, and protection. In countries like India, UNICEF plays a crucial role in reducing child mortality, improving maternal health, promoting early childhood education, and ensuring immunization coverage. It also focuses on safeguarding children from violence, exploitation, and abuse. During emergencies or natural disasters, UNICEF provides immediate relief such as food, clean water, and shelter, while also supporting long-term recovery efforts. Through advocacy, technical support, and on-ground programs, UNICEF works to create a world where every child can thrive.

- **Child Rights:** UNICEF advocates for child rights, including education, health, and protection.
- **Education:** UNICEF supports programs that improve access to quality education, particularly for disadvantaged children.
- **Emergency Response:** UNICEF provides humanitarian assistance to children affected by conflicts and natural disasters.

ROLE OF UNESCO (UNITED NATIONS EDUCATIONAL, SCIENTIFIC AND CULTURAL ORGANIZATION)

UNESCO plays a central role in promoting global peace and sustainable development through education, science, culture, and communication. Its primary aim is to build inclusive knowledge societies and foster intercultural dialogue by strengthening education systems, preserving cultural heritage, and promoting freedom of expression.In the field of education, UNESCO sets international standards and supports countries in policy-making, curriculum development, and teacher training to achieve quality and equitable education for all. It also promotes literacy, lifelong learning, and gender equality in education. In science, UNESCO encourages scientific cooperation, research, and the responsible use of technology for sustainable development. Culturally, it works to protect world heritage sites and promote cultural diversity. In countries like India, UNESCO supports initiatives in digital learning, cultural preservation, and inclusive education, making significant contributions to national and community development.

- **Education for All:** UNESCO promotes Education for All (EFA) initiatives, aiming to ensure every child has access to quality education.

- **Cultural Diversity:** UNESCO celebrates cultural diversity and promotes intercultural dialogue through education and cultural programs.
- **Sustainable Development:** UNESCO supports sustainable development through education, science, and culture.

ROLE OF NON-GOVERNMENTAL ORGANIZATIONS (NGO)

Non-Governmental Organizations (NGOs) play a vital role in social development by filling gaps in government services and advocating for the rights of marginalized communities. They work at local, national, and international levels across various sectors such as education, health, environment, child welfare, women's empowerment, and poverty alleviation. NGOs are often more flexible and responsive than government agencies, allowing them to innovate and adapt quickly to community needs. In India, NGOs like Pratham, CRY, Smile Foundation, and Akshaya Patra have been instrumental in improving literacy, child protection, and nutrition. They also work to raise awareness, build community capacity, and ensure participation in development programs. NGOs often collaborate with governments, international organizations, and the private sector to implement projects and influence policy.

Their grassroots presence enables them to build trust with communities and drive meaningful, sustainable change.

- **Community Development:** NGOs work at the grassroots level, promoting community development and empowerment.
- **Education and Skills:** NGOs provide education and skills training to marginalized communities.
- **Advocacy:** NGOs advocate for policy changes and human rights, including education and social justice.

ROLE OF SELF-HELP GROUPS (SHG)

Self-Help Groups (SHGs) are small, voluntary associations of people—typically women—from similar socio-economic backgrounds who come together to save money, access credit, and support one another in financial and social development. SHGs play a crucial role in empowering women, promoting financial inclusion, and improving livelihoods in rural and semi-urban areas. These groups function as informal banks, enabling members to pool savings and provide loans for small businesses, health emergencies, education, or other personal needs. Supported by initiatives like the National Rural Livelihood Mission (NRLM), SHGs receive training, access to microfinance, and linkages to banks and government schemes. Beyond financial benefits, SHGs encourage leadership, collective decision-making, and active participation in local governance. They often collaborate with Gram Panchayats and NGOs to implement community development projects, making them powerful agents of grassroots change.

- **Women's Empowerment:** SHGs empower women through microfinance, skills training, and collective action.
- **Community Development:** SHGs promote community development and social cohesion.
- **Financial Inclusion:** SHGs provide financial services to members, promoting financial inclusion.

ROLE OF ICDS AND ECCE

Integrated Child Development Services (ICDS) is a flagship program launched by the Government of India to address the health, nutrition, and development needs of children under the age of six and their mothers. Delivered primarily through Anganwadi centres, ICDS provides a comprehensive package of services including supplementary nutrition, immunization, health check-ups, referral services, pre-school education, and health and nutrition education for mothers. Its goal is to combat child malnutrition, reduce infant mortality, and lay a strong foundation for lifelong learning and development.Early Childhood Care and Education (ECCE) focuses on the holistic development of children from birth to eight years of age. It emphasizes nurturing care, early learning, good health, and proper nutrition during the most critical phase of human development. ECCE programs aim to ensure children are school-ready by supporting cognitive, emotional, social, and physical growth. Under India's National Education Policy (NEP) 2020, ECCE has been made an integral part of the education system, recognizing its importance in shaping a child's future learning outcomes.Together, ICDS and ECCE work to ensure that children receive the care, nourishment, and early education they need for healthy development, especially in rural and disadvantaged areas.

- **Early Childhood Development:** ICDS and ECCE programs focus on early childhood development, providing nutrition, health, and education services.
- **Holistic Development:** These programs promote holistic development of children, including physical, emotional, and cognitive development.
- **Community-Based:** ICDS and ECCE programs are often community-based, involving local participation and ownership.

ROLE OF GRAM PANCHAYATS

Gram Panchayats are the basic units of local self-government in rural India and play a key role in grassroots democracy and rural development.

As elected bodies at the village level, they are responsible for implementing government schemes and ensuring the delivery of essential services such as sanitation, drinking water, rural housing, education, health, and infrastructure.

Gram Panchayats serve as a link between the government and the community, allowing villagers to participate directly in decision-making processes. They prepare and execute development plans, manage local resources, and maintain records related to births, deaths, and land ownership. Gram Panchayats also play an important role in social welfare by supporting programs related to women and child development, self-help groups (SHGs), Integrated Child Development Services (ICDS), and Early Childhood Care and Education (ECCE).By promoting transparency, accountability, and community participation, Gram Panchayats help ensure that development is inclusive and tailored to the specific needs of each village. Their involvement is crucial in building empowered, self-reliant rural communities.

- **Local Governance:** Gram Panchayats are responsible for local governance, including education, health, and infrastructure development.
- **Community Development:** Gram Panchayats promote community development and social welfare.
- **Participatory Decision-Making:** Gram Panchayats involve local communities in decision-making processes, ensuring participatory governance.

PROGRAMMES FOR WOMEN EMPOWERMENT

Programs for women empowerment in India have played a significant role in promoting gender equality, enhancing women's status, and enabling them to participate actively in social, economic, and political life. One such program is the Mahila Samakhya Programme, launched in 1989 with the aim of empowering rural women through education and awareness. It focused on forming collectives called Sanghas where women could come together to discuss their rights, challenge social norms, and participate in local governance. By fostering confidence, leadership, and decision-making abilities, Mahila Samakhya helped many women move from the margins to the mainstream of society.

Adolescence being a critical stage in a girl's life, the government introduced the Kishori Shakti Yojana (KSY) under the Integrated Child Development Services (ICDS) to address the needs of girls aged 11-18 years. This scheme aimed to improve the nutritional and health status of adolescent girls, enhance their self-development skills, and promote awareness about hygiene, reproductive health, and family welfare. Through vocational training and life skills education, KSY aimed to delay early marriages, reduce school dropout rates, and prepare girls for responsible adulthood. In 2010, the Rajiv Gandhi Scheme for Empowerment of Adolescent Girls, also known as SABLA, was launched to strengthen the impact of earlier schemes like KSY. Targeting the same age group, SABLA provided an integrated package of services including health check-ups, supplementary nutrition, life skills, counselling, and vocational training, delivered mainly through Anganwadi centres. It focused on equipping girls with the knowledge and skills necessary to become independent, confident, and informed individuals capable of contributing to their families and communities.

These programs, taken together, reflect a holistic approach to women's empowerment by addressing different life stages and socio-economic challenges. By focusing on education, health, skill development, and awareness, they aim to break the cycle of gender discrimination and enable women and girls to lead dignified and productive lives. Their successful implementation has not only improved the quality of life for millions but also contributed to the broader goals of social justice and national development.

MAHILA SAMAKHYA PROGRAMME – A STEP TOWARD WOMEN EMPOWERMENT

The Mahila Samakhya Programme was launched in 1989 by the Government of India as a flagship initiative to empower rural women, particularly those from marginalized communities. Rooted in the belief that education is a powerful tool for social change, the program aimed to bring about women's empowerment through education, awareness, and collective action. It was implemented in partnership with state governments and focused on enhancing women's self-confidence, creating awareness about their rights, and encouraging participation in local governance and decision-making. A key feature of Mahila Samakhya was the formation of Sanghas - women's collectives at the village level. These collectives provided a platform for women to meet regularly, share their experiences, and discuss issues affecting their lives such as gender discrimination, health, violence, child marriage, and illiteracy. Through these discussions, women not only developed leadership and communication skills but also mobilized to demand services and entitlements from public institutions, including education, healthcare, and social welfare schemes.

The program also facilitated functional literacy, vocational training, legal awareness, and support for income-generating activities. Many Sanghas took initiatives to start community schools, fight domestic violence, and ensure girls' enrolment and retention in schools. Over time, Mahila Samakhya helped transform women from passive recipients of aid into active agents of change, who influenced decisions in families, communities, and even in local governance bodies like Panchayats. Overall, Mahila Samakhya proved to be a transformative movement in India's efforts toward gender equality. Although it was phased out in 2016 and integrated into other schemes, its legacy continues to inspire grassroots women's movements and remains a model for participatory, education-driven empowerment.

KISHORI SHAKTI YOJANA – EMPOWERING ADOLESCENT GIRLS

Kishori Shakti Yojana (KSY) is a centrally sponsored scheme launched by the Government of India under the Integrated Child Development Services (ICDS) to empower adolescent girls aged 11 to 18 years. The program aims to improve the nutritional and health status of girls, enhance their self-development skills, and provide awareness on key issues such as hygiene, reproductive health, family welfare, and education. By addressing both the physical and emotional needs of adolescent girls, KSY seeks to prepare them for a healthy and productive life. One of the major objectives of the scheme is to reduce the incidence of early marriages and school dropouts among girls. It also promotes skill development and vocational training to make girls economically self-reliant. Through these efforts, KSY empowers adolescent girls to make informed decisions and take control of their futures. The scheme also emphasizes the importance of life skills education to help girls deal with social pressures and challenges during adolescence.

KSY is implemented through Anganwadi centres, where selected adolescent girls are enrolled and receive services such as supplementary nutrition, health check-ups, counselling, and non-formal education. The program also involves community-based activities and awareness campaigns to promote gender equality and support girls' rights. Parents and community members are engaged to foster a supportive environment for adolescent development. Overall, Kishori Shakti Yojana plays a vital role in empowering young girls, especially in rural and underprivileged areas. By focusing on their overall well-being and development, the scheme helps create a strong foundation for future women leaders, professionals, and change-makers in society.

RAJIV GANDHI SCHEME FOR EMPOWERMENT OF ADOLESCENT GIRLS (SABLA)

The Rajiv Gandhi Scheme for Empowerment of Adolescent Girls, popularly known as SABLA, was launched by the Government of India in 2010 to address the multidimensional needs of adolescent girls aged 11 to 18 years. Replacing the earlier Kishori Shakti Yojana in selected districts,

SABLA aimed to empower girls through a combination of nutrition, health education, life skills, and vocational training. The program was designed to equip adolescent girls with the tools and knowledge necessary for leading a healthy, informed, and independent life.Implemented through Anganwadi centres under the Integrated Child Development Services (ICDS), SABLA provides two main components: nutrition and non-nutrition services. The nutrition component includes the provision of take-home rations or hot cooked meals for out-of-school girls, while the non-nutrition component includes health check-ups, counselling, adolescent reproductive and sexual health education, life skills, and vocational training. The scheme pays special attention to vulnerable groups, including out-of-school girls and those in marginalized communities.

SABLA also focuses on promoting school retention, delaying the age of marriage, and building awareness about social and legal rights. Community mobilization and parental involvement are key elements in ensuring the effectiveness of the program. Regular monitoring and collaboration with health, education, and skill development departments help in delivering integrated services. By investing in adolescent girls during this critical stage of growth, SABLA plays a crucial role in breaking the cycle of poverty, discrimination, and poor health. It fosters confidence, self-reliance, and active participation in community and national development, thereby contributing significantly to the broader goal of women empowerment in India.

COMMUNITY-BASED PROGRAMMES

Community-based programmes are initiatives designed to empower individuals and groups at the grassroots level by involving them directly in planning, decision-making, and implementation processes. These programmes aim to address local issues through participatory approaches, ensuring that solutions are relevant, sustainable, and culturally appropriate. They typically focus on areas such as health, education, livelihood, sanitation, women and child development, and environmental conservation.One prominent example is the Integrated Child Development Services (ICDS), which operates through Anganwadi centres in villages to deliver health, nutrition, and early education services to mothers and young children. Similarly, Self-Help Groups (SHGs) engage women in savings and credit activities, encouraging economic independence and social empowerment. These groups often lead to broader community development by supporting local enterprises, health awareness, and educational outreach.

Another key community-based effort is the National Rural Health Mission (NRHM), which uses Accredited Social Health Activists (ASHAs) to provide basic health care and promote health-seeking behaviour in rural areas. Environmental programmes like Swachh Bharat Abhiyan (Clean India Mission) also rely heavily on community participation to improve sanitation and hygiene standards in both rural and urban areas. Overall, community-based programmes create a sense of ownership and responsibility among local people, enabling them to actively contribute to their own development. By fostering collaboration between government, NGOs, and the community, these programmes are vital in achieving inclusive and sustainable growth.

Types of Community-Based Programs

- **Health Programs:** Community-based health programs focus on promoting health awareness, providing healthcare services, and improving health outcomes.
- **Education Programs:** Community-based education programs aim to improve access to education, promote literacy, and enhance educational outcomes.
- **Livelihood Programs:** Community-based livelihood programs focus on promoting economic development, improving livelihoods, and enhancing income-generating opportunities.
- **Women's Empowerment Programs:** Community-based women's empowerment programs aim to promote women's rights, empower women, and improve their socio-economic status.

Benefits of Community-Based Programs

- **Increased Community Ownership:** Community-based programs promote community ownership and participation, leading to more effective and sustainable outcomes.
- **Improved Relevance:** Community-based programs are more relevant to the specific needs and context of the community.
- **Enhanced Sustainability:** Community-based programs are more likely to be sustainable in the long term, as they are driven by community needs and priorities.
- **Increased Impact:** Community-based programs can have a greater impact on the community, as they are tailored to the specific needs and context of the community.

Examples of Community-Based Programs

- **Self-Help Groups (SHGs):** SHGs are community-based groups that promote economic development, social empowerment, and community participation.

- **Community Health Workers:** Community health workers are trained individuals who provide basic healthcare services and promote health awareness in their communities.

- **Community-Based Education Programs:** Community-based education programs, such as literacy programs and vocational training, aim to improve access to education and promote educational outcomes.
- **Women's Empowerment Initiatives:** Women's empowerment initiatives, such as microfinance programs and skills training, aim to promote women's rights and empower women.

Challenges and Limitations

- **Limited Resources:** Community-based programs often face limited resources, including funding, infrastructure, and personnel.
- **Community Engagement:** Community-based programs require active community engagement and participation, which can be challenging to achieve.
- **Sustainability:** Community-based programs may face sustainability challenges, particularly if they rely on external funding or support.
- **Scalability:** Community-based programs may be difficult to scale up or replicate in other contexts, due to their specific nature and requirements.

Overall, community-based programs have the potential to promote social change, improve living standards, and empower communities. However, they require careful planning, implementation, and management to ensure their effectiveness and sustainability.

SUSTAINABLE LIVELIHOOD PRACTICES

Sustainable livelihood practices refer to methods and approaches that enable individuals and communities to meet their basic needs and improve their quality of life without depleting natural resources or harming the environment. These practices focus on long-term economic stability, environmental protection, and social equity. They are particularly significant in rural and marginalized communities where livelihoods are closely linked to natural resources like land, water, and forests.Examples of sustainable livelihood practices include organic farming, water harvesting, agroforestry, and eco-friendly handicrafts. Organic farming avoids the use of chemical fertilizers and pesticides, preserving soil health and biodiversity. Agroforestry combines agriculture and tree cultivation, offering income diversity and improving ecological balance. Similarly, promoting non-timber forest products (NTFPs) allows forest-dependent communities to earn income without harming forest ecosystems.

Many of these practices are supported by initiatives such as the National Rural Livelihoods Mission (NRLM) and various NGO-led livelihood programs that provide training, financial support, and market access. These programs often integrate local knowledge and promote community ownership, ensuring that the solutions are culturally appropriate and economically viable over the long term. Sustainable livelihoods are essential for achieving both poverty reduction and environmental conservation. By focusing on resource-efficient, resilient, and inclusive development, these practices help communities become self-reliant while protecting the planet for future generations.

Key Principles of Sustainable Livelihood Practices

- **Environmental Sustainability:** Conservation and sustainable use of natural resources.
- **Social Equity:** Fair distribution of benefits and opportunities among all members of the community.
- **Economic Viability:** Sustainable and profitable economic activities that benefit local communities.
- **Human Well-being:** Improvement of living standards, health, and overall well-being of individuals and communities.

Examples of Sustainable Livelihood Practices

- **Organic Farming:** Farming practices that avoid the use of synthetic fertilizers and pesticides, promoting soil health and biodiversity.
- **Sustainable Agriculture:** Agricultural practices that conserve natural resources, reduce waste, and promote ecosystem services.
- **Eco-Tourism:** Tourism that promotes conservation of natural resources and cultural heritage, while generating income for local communities.
- **Renewable Energy:** Use of renewable energy sources, such as solar and wind power, to reduce dependence on fossil fuels and mitigate climate change.
- **Community-Based Forest Management:** Community-led management of forests, promoting sustainable forest management and equitable benefit-sharing.

Benefits of Sustainable Livelihood Practices

- **Improved Livelihoods:** Sustainable livelihood practices can improve income, food security, and overall well-being of individuals and communities.
- **Environmental Conservation:** Sustainable practices can conserve natural resources, reduce pollution, and mitigate climate change.
- **Social Equity:** Sustainable livelihood practices can promote social equity, reduce poverty, and improve human rights.

- **Economic Benefits:** Sustainable practices can generate economic benefits, create jobs, and stimulate local economies.

Challenges and Limitations

- **Limited Access to Markets:** Limited access to markets, credit, and other resources can hinder the adoption of sustainable livelihood practices.
- **Lack of Awareness:** Limited awareness and understanding of sustainable livelihood practices can limit their adoption.
- **Policy and Regulatory Frameworks:** Inadequate policy and regulatory frameworks can hinder the promotion of sustainable livelihood practices.
- **Climate Change:** Climate change can impact the sustainability of livelihood practices, requiring adaptation and resilience-building strategies.

Overall, sustainable livelihood practices offer a promising approach to promoting economic development, social equity, and environmental sustainability. By adopting these practices, individuals and communities can improve their livelihoods while contributing to a more sustainable future.

MINORITY SCHOLARSHIPS – GOVERNMENT AND NGO INITIATIVES

Minority scholarships are targeted efforts to support the educational advancement of students belonging to minority communities such as Muslims, Christians, Sikhs, Buddhists, Parsis, and Jains. These scholarships, provided by both government bodies and non-governmental organizations (NGOs), aim to reduce educational inequality and promote inclusive development by assisting students from economically and socially marginalized sections of society. The Government of India, through the Ministry of Minority Affairs, offers several key scholarships under the Prime Minister's New 15-Point Programme for the Welfare of Minorities. These include the Pre-Matric Scholarship, Post-Matric Scholarship, and Merit-cum-Means Scholarship for professional and technical courses. These schemes cover school fees, maintenance allowances, and other education-related expenses for minority students from Class 1 to postgraduate level. The scholarships are disbursed through the National Scholarship Portal (NSP), ensuring transparency and accessibility.

NGOs also play a significant role in providing scholarships to minority students. Organizations such as the Maulana Azad Education Foundation offer educational support to minority girls through the Begum Hazrat Mahal National Scholarship. Other NGOs like Zakat Foundation of India, Help India Foundation, and Foundation for Academic Excellence and Access (FAEA) provide financial aid, mentoring, and career support to talented minority students pursuing higher education in India and abroad. Together, government and NGO-based minority scholarships address barriers such as financial hardship, lack of access, and low representation in higher education. By empowering students from minority communities, these initiatives promote social inclusion, educational equity, and national development.

GOVERNMENT SCHOLARSHIPS

The Indian government provides numerous scholarships to support minority students across the country. These scholarships are primarily administered by the Ministry of Minority Affairs and are available to students from communities like Muslims, Sikhs, Christians, Buddhists, Parsis, and Jains.

Pre-Matric Scholarship Scheme for Minorities

- **Eligibility:** Students from minority communities studying in classes I to X.
- **Academic Requirement:** Minimum of 50% marks in the previous final examination.
- **Income Limit:** Annual family income should not exceed 1 lakh.
- **Domicile:** Must be an Indian citizen.
- **Application Portal:** National Scholarship Portal

Post-Matric Scholarship Scheme for Minorities

- **Eligibility:** Students from minority communities pursuing studies from Class XI to Ph.D.
- **Academic Requirement:** Minimum of 50% marks in the last final examination.
- **Income Limit:** Annual family income should not exceed 2 lakh.
- **Application Portal:** National Scholarship Portal.

Merit-Cum-Means Scholarship Scheme for Professional and Technical Courses

- **Eligibility:** Minority students pursuing professional and technical courses.
- **Academic Requirement:** Minimum of 50% marks in the last qualifying examination.
- **Income Limit:** Annual family income should not exceed 2.5 lakh.
- **Domicile:** Indian citizens.
- **Application Portal:** National Scholarship Portal

Naya Savera – Free Coaching for Civil Services Examination

- **Eligibility:** Minority students who have completed graduation and wish to appear for civil services exams.
- **Academic Requirement:** Graduation with a minimum of 50% marks.
- **Income Limit:** Annual family income should not exceed 6 lakh.
- **Application Portal:** Ministry of Minority Affairs.

NGO SCHOLARSHIPS

NGOs also play a vital role in providing scholarships to minority students, particularly those who need financial assistance for higher education or special courses. These scholarships may also include mentorship and career support, in addition to financial aid.

Sitaram Jindal Foundation Scholarship

- **Eligibility:** Students from underprivileged backgrounds pursuing education from Class 11 to postgraduate level.
- **Academic Requirement:** For Class 11 students, a minimum of 60% marks in the previous examination.
- **Income Limit:** Annual family income should not exceed 2.5 lakh.
- **Application Portal:** Sitaram Jindal Foundation.

Aga Khan Foundation International Scholarship

- **Eligibility:** Students pursuing master's level courses in various fields, including education, health, and development.
- **Academic Requirement:** Excellent academic record.
- **Income Limit:** Preference is given to those demonstrating financial need.
- **Application Portal:** Aga Khan Foundation.

Maulana Azad Education Foundation (MAEF) Scholarship

- **Eligibility:** Minority girls who wish to pursue higher education, particularly in professional and technical courses.
- **Academic Requirement:** Minimum of 50% marks in the last qualifying examination.
- **Income Limit:** Annual family income should not exceed 2 lakh.
- **Application Portal:** Maulana Azad Education Foundation.

Zakat Foundation of India Scholarship

- **Eligibility:** Minority students from economically weaker sections pursuing education from school to college and higher studies.

- **Income Limit:** Annual family income should not exceed 5 lakh.
- **Application Portal:** Zakat Foundation of India.

Help India Foundation Scholarship

- **Eligibility:** Students from marginalized communities pursuing higher education.
- **Academic Requirement:** Minimum of 50% marks in the last qualifying examination.
- **Income Limit:** Annual family income should not exceed 3 lakh.
- **Application Portal:** Help India Foundation

Application Process

To apply for these scholarships, students need to visit the respective portals and submit their applications along with the required documents, including proof of income, academic records, and identity proof.

- **Government Scholarships:** Applications can be submitted via National Scholarship Portal (NSP).
- **NGO Scholarships:** Applicants should visit the respective NGO's official website for detailed application procedures.

CONCLUSION

The role of various international agencies such as UNDP, UNICEF, and UNESCO, along with national bodies, local governance structures, and community-based organizations, is pivotal in promoting sustainable development and empowering marginalized communities, particularly women and children. These agencies have played a central role in addressing inequalities and creating opportunities for underrepresented groups. Through their efforts in education, healthcare, economic empowerment, and advocacy, they have brought attention to the systemic challenges faced by women and children and have driven significant changes at both the policy and grassroots levels.UNDP's focus on human development and eradicating poverty through sustainable solutions has been instrumental in advancing gender equality and women's participation in economic activities. Their support for capacity building, infrastructure development, and policy reform has enabled governments to implement effective strategies for empowerment. Similarly, UNICEF's programs on child protection, education, and nutrition have ensured that vulnerable children, especially girls, have access to the essential resources for their development and well-being.UNESCO's contributions to education, especially through its emphasis on inclusive and equitable access to quality education, have strengthened the efforts of nations to empower women through learning. By advocating for gender-sensitive educational policies and programs, UNESCO has helped to reduce barriers to education for girls and women, fostering their active participation in social and economic life. This, in turn, has contributed to the broader goal of gender equality and the empowerment of women.Non-Governmental Organizations (NGOs) have had a unique role in transforming local communities by providing targeted interventions where government programs may not have had reach. Their work in areas such as health, education, and economic development has been crucial in empowering women at the grassroots level. Through advocacy, capacity building, and direct service delivery, NGOs help bridge gaps in access to services and resources, ensuring that women and marginalized groups are not left behind.

Self-Help Groups (SHGs) have been one of the most effective grassroots initiatives for women empowerment, particularly in rural areas. By providing women with the opportunity to engage in collective economic activities, SHGs foster a sense of agency and leadership. These groups not only improve financial independence but also serve as platforms for women to share knowledge, support one another, and collectively address social issues like domestic violence and health problems. The success of SHGs demonstrates the transformative potential of community-driven efforts in advancing women's empowerment. The Integrated Child Development Services (ICDS) and Early Childhood Care and Education (ECCE) programs have made a substantial impact in improving the well-being of children, especially in marginalized communities. By providing a holistic package of services, including health, nutrition, education, and social services, these programs have not only contributed to the health and development of children but also created opportunities for women to access essential services and improve their own lives. The integrated approach of ICDS and ECCE is essential in fostering long-term social change.

The government's specific programs for women empowerment, such as Mahila Samakhya, Kishori Shakti Yojana, and the Rajiv Gandhi Scheme for Empowerment of Adolescent Girls, have proven to be critical in addressing the multifaceted needs of women and girls. These programs provide educational support, skills training, and health services, empowering women and girls to make informed decisions about their lives and contribute to society's progress. These targeted interventions are especially significant in rural areas, where women face significant barriers to empowerment.Community-based programs have been crucial in achieving sustainable development. By involving local people in identifying their needs and designing solutions, these programs ensure that interventions are culturally relevant and locally accepted. The success of these initiatives depends on strong community participation, which creates a sense of ownership and responsibility. Empowering local communities, particularly women, to become leaders in their development is one of the most effective ways to ensure the long-term sustainability of empowerment efforts.

Sustainable livelihood practices are fundamental to ensuring that women's economic empowerment is not just a short-term achievement but a lasting transformation. By promoting practices that are economically viable and environmentally sustainable, women gain the skills and resources necessary to improve their livelihoods without compromising the well-being of future generations. These practices enhance women's participation in economic activities, reduce dependence on external aid, and create more resilient communities.

The provision of minority scholarships by both the government and NGOs has been a crucial element in breaking down barriers to education for marginalized groups. These scholarships enable girls and boys from minority communities to pursue education, which serves as a pathway to personal and collective empowerment. By making education accessible to all, regardless of economic background, these initiatives contribute to a more just and equitable society, where all individuals, especially women and minorities, can contribute to and benefit from economic and social progress.

In conclusion, the combined efforts of international agencies, national programs, community-based organizations, and local governance structures have significantly advanced the empowerment of women, children, and marginalized groups. Through their integrated approach, these initiatives address not only immediate needs but also the long-term structural challenges that hinder social progress. As these efforts continue to evolve, it is crucial to maintain a focus on inclusive, sustainable, and gender-sensitive development, ensuring that all members of society have equal access to opportunities and resources. The journey towards a more equitable world is ongoing, but with continued collaboration and commitment, the vision of true empowerment for all is within reach.

KEY POINTS

- **Role of International and National Agencies:** UNDP focuses on poverty alleviation, gender equality, and capacity building by supporting sustainable development programs that uplift marginalized groups.UNICEF emphasizes child rights, education, health, and protection, particularly advocating for girls' education and maternal care. UNESCO promotes inclusive education, gender equality, and cultural development, empowering women through literacy and leadership initiatives.
- **Contribution of NGOs:** Non-Governmental Organizations (NGOs) play a key role in delivering education, healthcare, and economic opportunities to underserved populations. They bridge gaps between policy and practice, empower women through training, and enhance community participation.

- **Self-Help Groups (SHGs):** SHGs enable rural women to come together for savings and credit activities, helping them gain financial independence and social empowerment. They serve as platforms for awareness, solidarity, and grassroots leadership.
- **Integrated Child Development Services (ICDS) and ECCE:** ICDS provides nutrition, immunization, health checkups, and preschool education.ECCE (Early Childhood Care and Education) emphasizes the holistic development of children below 6 years and also supports working mothers, thus indirectly promoting women empowerment.
- **Role of Gram Panchayats:** Gram Panchayats serve as local self-governments and ensure grassroots democracy. Women's participation in panchayats has empowered them to take active roles in community development, policy-making, and resource allocation.
- **Government Schemes for Women Empowerment:** Mahila Samakhya: Focuses on collective action, literacy, and leadership training for rural women. Kishori Shakti Yojana: Aims to improve the nutritional, educational, and skill-based development of adolescent girls. Rajiv Gandhi Scheme for Empowerment of Adolescent Girls (SABLA): Enhances the self-development, health, and well-being of adolescent girls through education and vocational training.
- **Community-Based Programmes:** These are participatory models involving local stakeholders to address social issues. Programs often focus on education, health, sanitation, and economic empowerment, with special attention to the needs of women and children.
- **Sustainable Livelihood Practices:** Sustainable practices promote economic self-reliance for women through eco-friendly and income-generating activities like organic farming, handicrafts, and small-scale entrepreneurship. These practices ensure long-term financial security and environmental conservation.
- **Minority Scholarships – Government and NGOs:** Government and NGO-funded scholarships support minority students, especially girls, to continue their education and skill development. These scholarships aim to reduce dropout rates and promote equity in educational attainment.

The collective impact of these agencies, programs, and practices has been substantial in transforming the socio-economic conditions of women and children. By focusing on education, health, financial independence, and community participation, these initiatives promote inclusive growth and long-term empowerment.

REFERENCES

1. Aga Khan Foundation. (2023). *Aga Khan International Scholarship Program.* https://www.akdn.org
2. Chambers, R., & Conway, G. (1992). *Sustainable Rural Livelihoods: Practical Concepts for the 21st century* (IDS Discussion Paper 296). Institute of Development Studies. https://opendocs.ids.ac.uk/opendocs/handle/20.500.12413/775
3. FAO. (2018). *Agroforestry for Sustainable Agriculture.* Food and Agriculture Organization of the United Nations. https://www.fao.org
4. Foundation for Academic Excellence and Access (FAEA). (2023). *Scholarship Program for Minority and Disadvantaged Students.* https://www.faeaindia.org
5. Government of India. (2016). *Annual Report on Integrated Child Development Services (ICDS).* Ministry of Women and Child Development. https://www.wcd.nic.in
6. Help India Foundation. (2022). *Educational Support and Scholarships.* https://helpindiafoundation.in
7. International Fund for Agricultural Development (IFAD). (2012). *Sustainable Livelihoods Approach.* https://www.ifad.org/en/web/knowledge/-/publication/sustainable-livelihoods-approach
8. Maulana Azad Education Foundation. (2022). *Begum Hazrat Mahal National Scholarship for minority girls.* https://maef.nic.in
9. Maulana Azad Education Foundation. (2022). *Maulana Azad Scholarship for Minority girls.* https://maef.nic.in
10. Ministry of Drinking Water and Sanitation. (2017). *Swachh Bharat Mission (Gramin): Guidelines.* Government of India. https://swachhbharatmission.gov.in
11. Ministry of Health and Family Welfare. (2013). *National Rural Health Mission: Framework for Implementation.* Government of India. https://nhm.gov.in
12. Ministry of Minority Affairs. (2023). *Post-matric Scholarship Scheme for Minorities.* Government of India. https://scholarships.gov.in
13. Ministry of Minority Affairs. (2023). *Pre-matric Scholarship Scheme for Minorities.* Government of India. https://scholarships.gov.in
14. Ministry of Minority Affairs. (2023). *Scholarship Schemes for Minority Communities.* Government of India. https://minorityaffairs.gov.in
15. Ministry of Rural Development. (2013). *National Rural Livelihoods Mission (NRLM): Framework for Implementation.* Government of India. https://aajeevika.gov.in
16. Ministry of Women and Child Development. (2008). *Kishori Shakti Yojana: Guidelines for Implementation.* Government of India. https://wcd.nic.in/sites/default/files/ksyguidelines.pdf
17. Ministry of Women and Child Development. (2010). *Rajiv Gandhi Scheme for Empowerment of Adolescent Girls (SABLA) – Guidelines for Implementation.* Government of India. https://wcd.nic.in

18. Ministry of Women and Child Development. (2013). *Mahila Samakhya Programme: An overview*. Government of India. https://wcd.nic.in
19. Ministry of Women and Child Development. (2014). *Integrated Child Development Services (ICDS): Scheme Overview*. Government of India. https://wcd.nic.in
20. National Rural Livelihoods Mission (NRLM). (n.d.). *Self-help Groups and their Role in Rural Development*. Ministry of Rural Development, Government of India. https://aajeevika.gov.in
21. National Scholarship Portal. (2023). *Minority Scholarships: Pre-matric, Post-matric, and Merit-cum-means*. Government of India. https://scholarships.gov.in
22. Planning Commission of India. (2011). *Evaluation Study on Mahila Samakhya Programme*. Government of India. https://niti.gov.in/planning commission.gov.in
23. Pratham. (n.d.). *About Pratham: Empowering Children through Education*. Pratham Education Foundation. https://www.pratham.org
24. Press Information Bureau. (2010). *Government Launches SABLA – A Scheme for Empowerment of Adolescent Girls*. https://pib.gov.in
25. UNDP. (n.d.). *What we do*. United Nations Development Programme. https://www.undp.org
26. UNDP India. (2019). *Sustainable Livelihoods: Empowering Communities and Strengthening Resilience*. United Nations Development Programme. https://www.in.undp.org
27. UNESCO. (2020). *Education for Sustainable Development*. United Nations Educational, Scientific and Cultural Organization. https://www.unesco.org/en/education
28. UNICEF. (2020). *UNICEF's Work*. United Nations Children's Fund. https://www.unicef.org
29. UNICEF India. (2018). *Empowering Communities through Community-based Programs*. https://www.unicef.org/india
30. Zakat Foundation of India. (2023). *Scholarship and Education Support Programs*. https://www.zakatindia.org
31. Zakat Foundation of India. (2023). *Scholarships for Minority Students*. https://www.zakatindia.org

6 CHAPTER

Research Priorities

INTRODUCTION

Education is a powerful tool for social transformation, particularly for marginalized communities such as Scheduled Castes (SCs), Scheduled Tribes (STs), girls, minorities, and other disadvantaged groups. In India, the government has initiated several centrally sponsored schemes aimed at addressing the educational gaps and promoting inclusive development. These efforts reflect a commitment to ensuring that every child, regardless of background, has equal access to quality education and opportunities for personal and academic growth.Centrally sponsored schemes for the education of SCs and STs, such as the Pre-Matric and Post-Matric Scholarships, Ashram Schools, and Hostels for ST boys and girls, are designed to reduce dropout rates and support academic continuity. These schemes aim to eliminate economic barriers, improve infrastructure in tribal areas, and provide additional academic support to marginalized students. Similarly, schemes for minorities such as the Maulana Azad National Fellowship and the Nai Udaan program focus on promoting higher education and skill development. For girls, especially those belonging to disadvantaged backgrounds, specific programs like the National Scheme of Incentive to Girls for Secondary Education (NSIGSE), and Beti Bachao Beti Padhao have been implemented. These schemes target both the economic and social constraints that hinder girls' education. By offering financial incentives, awareness campaigns, and improved facilities, they work towards creating a safe and supportive educational environment.

Despite these policy efforts, educational disparities persist, prompting the need for status studies that assess the actual conditions of education among SCs, STs, girls, minorities, and other marginalized groups. These studies provide valuable data on enrolment rates, retention, learning outcomes, and access to infrastructure. They also highlight systemic issues such as caste-based discrimination, gender bias, and socio-economic obstacles that prevent equitable participation in education. Teaching-learning practices and the degree of social inclusion in classrooms play a crucial role in shaping the educational experience of marginalized students. Inclusive pedagogy, teacher sensitization, language support, and culturally relevant curriculum are essential to ensure that all children feel respected and valued. However, there are challenges in effectively implementing these practices across all schools, especially in rural and under-resourced settings.

Social inclusion in education requires more than policyit demands a shift in school culture, teacher attitudes, and community engagement. Classrooms that promote equity and respect help students from marginalized backgrounds build confidence and achieve better outcomes. Training teachers to handle diversity sensitively and adopting student-centred pedagogies are vital steps toward achieving truly inclusive education. Innovative institutional practices have emerged as successful models for inclusive education. The Navodaya Vidyalaya Samithi, for instance, provides quality education to talented students from rural areas through residential schooling, fostering academic excellence and social integration. Its admission policy ensures representation of SCs, STs, and girls, promoting equity in access to quality education. The Kasturba Gandhi Balika Vidyalaya (KGBV) scheme addresses the educational needs of girls from disadvantaged communities by providing residential schooling at the upper primary level. These schools not only offer academic support but also address safety, health, and socio-emotional development—factors crucial for retaining girls in the education system. Institutions like the Maulana Azad National Foundation and traditional Madrassas have also played unique roles in minority education. While the Foundation provides scholarships and support services for Muslim girls and boys, some Madrassas have integrated mainstream education with religious instruction, helping bridge cultural and educational gaps. These efforts underscore the importance of culturally responsive education that respects and incorporates the identity of learners.

In short, the landscape of educational development for marginalized groups in India is shaped by a combination of centrally sponsored schemes, inclusive pedagogical practices, and innovative institutional models. While progress has been made, challenges remain in ensuring that all children receive equitable, quality education. Ongoing evaluation, community participation, and institutional innovation are critical to building an inclusive education system that leaves no one behind.

EVALUATION OF CENTRALLY SPONSORED EDUCATIONAL SCHEMES FOR MARGINALIZED COMMUNITIES IN INDIA

The Indian government has implemented several centrally sponsored schemes aimed at enhancing educational access and equity for marginalized communities, including Scheduled Castes (SCs), Scheduled Tribes (STs), girls, and minorities. These schemes are designed to reduce educational disparities, promote inclusivity, and provide financial and infrastructural support to underserved sections of society. Over the years, various ministries, particularly the Ministry of Education and the Ministry of Social Justice and Empowerment, have evaluated and revised these schemes to increase their effectiveness.

For SC and ST students, schemes such as the Post Matric Scholarship Scheme (PMS), Pre-Matric Scholarship Scheme, and Hostel facilities for SC/ST boys and girls have been pivotal. These programs aim to reduce dropout rates and support students in continuing their education beyond the secondary level. Evaluations reveal that while these schemes have positively influenced enrolment rates and reduced financial burdens, challenges persist in the timely disbursement of funds and awareness among beneficiaries. Monitoring mechanisms and digital platforms like the National Scholarship Portal have been introduced to streamline applications and improve transparency.

When it comes to girls' education, schemes like the Kasturba Gandhi Balika Vidyalaya (KGBV) and National Scheme of Incentive to Girls for Secondary Education (NSIGSE) have played significant roles. These programs aim to address gender disparities in education by providing residential schooling facilities and financial incentives to encourage girls, especially from SC/ST communities, to complete secondary education. Evaluations indicate increased retention and enrolment of girls, especially in rural and tribal areas. However, some studies suggest that greater focus on quality education, infrastructure improvements, and gender-sensitive curricula is still needed.

For minority communities, the Maulana Azad National Fellowship, Pre-Matric and Post-Matric Scholarships for Minorities, and the Nai Udaan scheme for civil services preparation have been instrumental. These initiatives aim to enhance educational participation among Muslims, Christians, Sikhs, Buddhists, Jains, and Parsis. Evaluations show a rise in educational attainment among minority groups, particularly in urban areas. Nevertheless, outreach in remote and backward regions remains a concern, pointing to the need for localized implementation and community engagement.

In summary, centrally sponsored schemes for the education of SCs, STs, girls, and minorities have made commendable progress in promoting educational equity. While enrollment and retention rates have improved, the real challenge lies in enhancing the quality of education, ensuring effective implementation, and building robust support systems that cater to the diverse needs of marginalized learners. Continued policy revisions, capacity building of implementing agencies, and active community participation are essential for the long-term success of these initiatives.The evaluation of centrally sponsored schemes for education of SCs, STs, girls, and minorities is a crucial step in assessing their effectiveness and impact. Here's what's happening:

Evaluation Process

The NITI Aayog's Development Monitoring and Evaluation Office (DMEO) has sought proposals from consultancy firms to support the evaluation of Centrally Sponsored Schemes (CSSs) focused on education and welfare of SCs, STs, minorities, and other vulnerable groups.

The evaluation will assess each scheme's relevance, effectiveness, and sustainability, with recommendations to either maintain, modify, or discontinue certain initiatives.

The consultancy firm will focus on optimizing resources and ensuring efficient use of government funds in future implementations.

Schemes Under Evaluation

- **Post Matric Scholarship for SCs:** A scheme providing financial assistance to SC students pursuing post-matric education.
- **Pradhan Mantri Anusuchit Jaati Abhyuday Yojana (PM AJAY):** A scheme aimed at improving the socio-economic conditions of SCs.
- **PM Young Achievers Scholarship Award Scheme for Vibrant India (PM YASASVI):** A scheme targeting OBCs, EBCs, and De-notified Tribes (DNTs).
- Other schemes, such as the Atal Vayo Abhyuday Yojana (AVYAY) and the National Action Plan for Drug Demand Reduction (NAPDDR), may also be evaluated.

Objectives

- To evaluate the impact and effectiveness of CSSs in promoting education and welfare of SCs, STs, minorities, and other vulnerable groups.
- To identify areas of improvement and provide recommendations for optimizing resources and ensuring efficient use of government funds.

- To assess the sustainability and relevance of CSSs in achieving their intended objectives.

Expected Outcomes

The evaluation is expected to provide valuable insights into the strengths and weaknesses of CSSs, helping policymakers make informed decisions about future implementations. The recommendations from the evaluation will likely focus on improving the effectiveness, efficiency, and sustainability of CSSs, ultimately benefiting the target groups.

STATUS OF EDUCATION AMONG MARGINALIZED GROUPS IN INDIA: CHALLENGES AND PROGRESS

The status of education among Scheduled Castes (SCs), Scheduled Tribes (STs), girls, minorities, and other marginalized groups in India reflects a complex interplay of progress and persistent challenges. Over the years, the Indian government, along with various non-governmental organizations, has undertaken extensive efforts to bridge the educational gap through inclusive policies, targeted schemes, and affirmative action. Despite these efforts, disparities in access, retention, quality, and outcomes of education among these groups continue to exist due to socio-economic barriers, cultural factors, and systemic inequalities.

For SCs and STs, access to primary and secondary education has improved significantly, with higher enrolment rates observed due to initiatives like the Right to Education (RTE) Act, mid-day meal programs, and scholarships. However, dropout rates remain high, especially at the secondary level, largely due to poverty, child labour, and discrimination within schools. Infrastructure in tribal areas is often inadequate, with a shortage of trained teachers and learning materials, further hindering educational attainment.

Girls from marginalized communities face a dual burden—gender discrimination compounded by caste or minority status. While schemes like Beti Bachao Beti Padhao and Kasturba Gandhi Balika Vidyalaya have encouraged greater participation of girls in schools, early marriage, domestic responsibilities, and safety concerns continue to limit their educational opportunities. The gender gap is particularly pronounced in higher education and STEM fields, indicating the need for continued interventions focusing on empowerment and safety in education.

Minority communities, especially Muslims, often lag in educational indicators compared to national averages. Factors such as low socio-economic status, lack of awareness about educational opportunities, and inadequate representation in quality institutions contribute to their educational backwardness. Although schemes like Aikyashree and the Merit-cum-Means Scholarship have been introduced, challenges related to outreach, implementation, and cultural sensitivity persist. Similarly, children with disabilities and those from nomadic or migrant families face neglect in the education system due to a lack of inclusive curricula and infrastructure.

In conclusion, while India has made commendable progress in expanding educational access, the status study of marginalized groups underscores the urgent need for equity-focused policies. Efforts must move beyond access and concentrate on improving the quality of education, addressing social prejudices, and ensuring that marginalized learners receive the support needed to succeed academically and socially. Only then can education truly serve as a transformative tool for social justice and inclusive development.The status of education for SCs, STs, girls, minorities, and other marginalized groups in India is a complex issue with varying degrees of progress and challenges.

Literacy Rates

- **SCs (Scheduled Castes):** The literacy rate among SCs is 37.41%, with significant variations across states. Kerala has the highest literacy rate among SCs at 79.66%, while Bihar has the lowest at 19.49%.
- **STs (Scheduled Tribes):** The literacy rate among STs is 29.60%, with Kerala having the highest rate at 57.22% and Andhra Pradesh having the lowest at 17.16%.
- **Girls and Women:** Female literacy rates are lower than male literacy rates across all groups. For SCs, the female literacy rate is 23.76%, while for STs, it's 18.19%.

Challenges

- **High Dropout Rates:** A significant number of SC and ST students drop out of school, with dropout rates varying from 30% to 88% across different states.
- **Inadequate Facilities:** Many schools in tribal areas lack proper infrastructure, and hostel facilities are often insufficient.
- **Teacher Absence:** Frequent absence of teachers in remote areas hampers the education of marginalized groups.
- **Language Barriers:** Tribal children often face difficulties due to the difference between their dialect and the medium of instruction in schools.
- **Cultural and Social Barriers:** Early marriage, traditional norms, and values can limit educational opportunities for girls and women from marginalized groups.

Government Initiatives

- **Reservations:** Seats are reserved for SCs, STs, and OBCs in educational institutions, including engineering and medical colleges.
- **Scholarships:** Pre-matric and post-matric scholarships are provided to SC and ST students to encourage education.
- **Hostel Facilities:** Hostels are constructed to provide accommodation for students from marginalized groups.
- **Special Coaching:** Free special coaching is provided to students aspiring for admission to professional courses or preparing for competitive examinations.

Way Forward

To improve the educational status of marginalized groups, it's essential to address the issues of infrastructure, teacher availability, and cultural sensitivity. Providing education in tribal dialects, recruiting teachers from marginalized groups, and fixing school timings according to local needs can help increase educational participation.

INCLUSIVE TEACHING-LEARNING PRACTICES: FOSTERING EQUITY AND SOCIAL JUSTICE IN EDUCATION

Teaching-learning practices and social inclusion are deeply interconnected aspects of education that play a vital role in creating equitable, engaging, and transformative learning environments. Social inclusion in education refers to the deliberate efforts made to ensure that all students—regardless of their socio-economic background, caste, gender, ethnicity, disability, or religion—are given equal opportunities to participate fully in the learning process. In this context, teaching-learning practices must evolve to be inclusive, responsive, and culturally sensitive to address the diverse needs of learners and reduce systemic barriers to learning.

Inclusive teaching practices emphasize the use of learner-centred methods such as group discussions, collaborative projects, experiential learning, and the integration of local knowledge systems. These methods not only enhance participation and engagement but also validate the lived experiences of marginalized students. Teachers are encouraged to use differentiated instruction strategies, including varied teaching materials and assessment methods, to cater to students with different learning styles and abilities. Additionally, using mother tongue or bilingual instruction in early grades can significantly improve learning outcomes for students from tribal and minority communities.

Social inclusion in classrooms also requires the cultivation of an environment of respect, empathy, and equality. This involves training teachers to recognize and counteract their biases, use inclusive language, and address discriminatory behaviours. Curriculum content should reflect the diversity of the student population and include narratives, histories, and contributions of marginalized groups to build a sense of belonging and pride. Furthermore, physical infrastructuresuch as ramps, gender-neutral toilets, and accessible learning aidsshould support the participation of students with disabilities and others facing physical barriers.

Despite policy-level interventions such as the Right to Education Act, Samagra Shiksha Abhiyan, and inclusive education policies under the National Education Policy (NEP) 2020, challenges remain in actual classroom implementation. Large class sizes, lack of trained inclusive education specialists, limited resources, and deep-rooted social prejudices hinder the effectiveness of inclusive teaching practices. Therefore, ongoing teacher training, community involvement, and monitoring mechanisms are essential to bridge these gaps and ensure that teaching-learning practices genuinely promote social inclusion.

In essence, the study of teaching-learning practices in the context of social inclusion reveals that inclusive education is not merely about access but about meaningful participation and learning. An inclusive approach transforms education into a powerful tool for social justice, enabling students from all backgrounds to thrive and contribute to a more equitable society.

Study of Teaching-Learning Practices and Social Inclusion

The study of teaching-learning practices and social inclusion is crucial in understanding how educational institutions can promote equity, diversity, and inclusivity. Here's an overview:

Teaching-Learning Practices

- **Inclusive Pedagogy:** Teaching methods that cater to diverse learning needs, abilities, and backgrounds.
- **Differentiated Instruction:** Tailoring instruction to meet the unique needs of students.
- **Culturally Responsive Teaching:** Incorporating students' cultural backgrounds and experiences into the learning process.

Social Inclusion

- **Diverse and Inclusive Curriculum:** Curriculum that reflects the diversity of students' experiences, cultures, and backgrounds.
- **Inclusive Classroom Environment:** Creating a safe, welcoming, and respectful classroom environment that promotes social inclusion.
- **Teacher-Student Relationships:** Building positive relationships with students, particularly those from marginalized groups.

Benefits

- **Improved Academic Outcomes:** Inclusive teaching practices can lead to better academic outcomes for all students.
- **Increased Student Engagement:** Students are more likely to engage with learning when they feel included and valued.
- **Social-Emotional Learning:** Inclusive practices promote social-emotional learning, empathy, and understanding.

Challenges

- **Teacher Training:** Teachers may require training and support to develop inclusive teaching practices.
- **Cultural and Linguistic Diversity:** Teachers may face challenges in catering to students from diverse cultural and linguistic backgrounds.
- **Systemic Barriers:** Systemic barriers, such as inadequate resources and infrastructure, can hinder inclusive practices.

Strategies for Promoting Social Inclusion

- **Professional Development:** Providing teachers with training and support to develop inclusive teaching practices.
- **Curriculum Reform:** Reviewing and revising curriculum to ensure it is diverse and inclusive.
- **Community Engagement:** Engaging with local communities to promote diversity and inclusion.

By studying teaching-learning practices and social inclusion, educators can identify effective strategies to promote equity, diversity, and inclusivity in educational institutions.

INNOVATIVE INSTITUTIONAL PRACTICES IN INCLUSIVE EDUCATION: CASE STUDIES FROM NAVODAYA VIDYALAYA, KGBV, MAEF, AND MADRASSAS

Innovative institutional practices are critical for ensuring that education systems meet the diverse needs of learners, particularly in a country as socio-culturally complex as India. Various government-supported and community-rooted institutions have pioneered inclusive, equitable, and quality education through unique and context-specific models. Among these, Navodaya Vidyalaya Samithi (NVS), Kasturba Gandhi Balika Vidyalaya (KGBV), Maulana Azad Education Foundation (MAEF), and Madrassas stand out for their innovative practices in addressing access, quality, and social inclusion.

Navodaya Vidyalaya Samithi (NVS) operates a network of residential schools, known as Jawahar Navodaya Vidyalayas (JNVs), catering to talented children predominantly from rural areas. Established under the National Policy on Education (1986), these schools provide free education from Class VI to XII, including boarding, uniforms, textbooks, and co-curricular opportunities. The innovation in NVS lies in its merit-based, non-verbal entrance examination that reduces language or regional bias, thus identifying intellectual potential irrespective of background. These schools not only aim for academic excellence but also promote national integration through an inter-regional migration scheme that allows students from different linguistic backgrounds to study in each other's regions. This exchange fosters cultural awareness and unity. With state-of-the-art infrastructure, well-qualified teachers, and a structured residential learning environment, NVS has consistently produced high academic results, with many students gaining admission to prestigious universities and professional institutions. It has become a model for equitable education that combines merit with inclusion.

Kasturba Gandhi Balika Vidyalaya (KGBV) is another exemplary initiative aimed at reducing gender disparity in education. Launched in 2004 under the Sarva Shiksha Abhiyan (now integrated under Samagra Shiksha), KGBVs are residential schools meant for girls from disadvantaged groups—SC, ST, OBC, and minorities—who are out of school or at risk of dropping out. These schools target adolescent girls in upper primary and secondary levels and provide not only academic instruction but also life skills training, vocational education, and gender sensitization. The innovation in KGBV lies in its community-centred approach, where local women are employed as wardens or teachers, enhancing trust and participation. Additionally, the curriculum integrates value education, health, and hygiene awareness. Regular counselling sessions, community outreach, and parental engagement have contributed to increased retention and transition of girls into higher education. KGBVs thus serve as safe spaces that foster both learning and empowerment for girls who would otherwise remain outside the formal education system.

Maulana Azad Education Foundation (MAEF), established by the Ministry of Minority Affairs, plays a pivotal role in advancing education among minority communities, especially Muslim girls. The Foundation offers scholarships, infrastructure support, and awareness programs. One of its flagship initiatives, the Begum Hazrat Mahal National Scholarship, provides financial assistance to meritorious minority girls from Class IX to XII. The innovation of MAEF lies in its use of digital platforms for scholarship applications and direct benefit transfers (DBT), ensuring transparency, efficiency, and accountability. Additionally, MAEF provides grants to NGOs and educational institutions for constructing schools and hostels in minority-dominated areas. It also engages in advocacy and sensitization drives to counter socio-cultural barriers to education. By aligning financial support with community engagement, MAEF addresses both the economic and cultural factors that hinder educational participation among minorities.

Madrassas, traditionally Islamic religious schools, have been central to education in many minority communities. While historically focused on religious instruction, many Madrassas have undergone reforms to integrate mainstream subjects such as science, mathematics, English, and computer literacy, especially under schemes like the Scheme for Providing Quality Education in Madrassas (SPQEM). This dual curriculum approach is innovative because it respects the cultural and religious identity of students while simultaneously preparing them for broader educational and career opportunities. Modernized Madrassas have begun using smart classrooms, digital tools, and continuous teacher training to improve instructional quality. Efforts have also been made to align Madrassa education with formal school certification systems, enabling students to transition into mainstream academic or vocational streams. Despite challenges in implementation and public perception, modernized Madrassas demonstrate how traditional institutions can evolve to meet contemporary educational demands while maintaining cultural relevance.

In conclusion, these institutions reflect a broad spectrum of innovative educational practices that are responsive to the social realities of India's marginalized populations. Navodaya Vidyalayas showcase how merit and rural inclusion can be harmonized; KGBVs highlight the power of gender-responsive residential education; MAEF emphasizes minority empowerment through strategic financial support; and Madrassas illustrate the blending of traditional and modern education. Collectively, these case studies offer valuable lessons in policy innovation, community participation, and the need for sustained investment in inclusive education models. Scaling up such practices and integrating them into national educational planning is essential for achieving the goal of "Education for All" in its truest sense.

Navodaya Vidyalaya Samiti

The Navodaya Vidyalaya Samiti (NVS) was established with the objective of providing quality education to talented children predominantly from rural areas, with a strong emphasis on nurturing and developing their abilities. These schools are fully residential and equipped with modern infrastructure and facilities to support academic and personal growth. A key feature of NVS is its merit-based selection process, ensuring that gifted students from various parts of the country are given an equal opportunity to excel. The curriculum places significant emphasis on science, mathematics, and English, while also promoting holistic development through sports and extracurricular activities.

Over the years, Navodaya Vidyalayas have made remarkable achievements by producing talented individuals who have gone on to succeed in diverse fields. They have played a vital role in bridging the rural-urban educational divide and in contributing to the overall development of rural India. The academic performance of students has consistently improved, and the system has created increased opportunities for students from disadvantaged backgrounds.

However, the Navodaya Vidyalayas also face certain challenges. Some schools still struggle with limited access to adequate resources and infrastructure, which can hinder the delivery of quality education. Additionally, the high expectations placed on students to perform well in academics and other areas can sometimes lead to undue pressure.

Kasturba Gandhi Balika Vidyalaya (KGBV)

The Kasturba Gandhi Balika Vidyalaya (KGBV) scheme was launched with the objective of providing quality education to girls from marginalized sections of society, particularly in rural areas with low female literacy rates. These residential schools offer free boarding, lodging, uniforms, and study materials, ensuring that financial barriers do not hinder access to education. The initiative specifically targets girls from Scheduled Castes (SC), Scheduled Tribes (ST), Other Backward Classes (OBC), and minority communities, as well as those living below the poverty line. KGBVs aim to bridge the gender gap in education and reduce dropout rates by creating a supportive and inclusive learning environment.

The program places strong emphasis on life skills education, vocational training, and the overall empowerment of girls. As a result, it has made a significant impact, with over 40 lakh girls having benefited from the scheme. Enrolment rates have improved considerably, and dropout rates have reportedly decreased by around 30%. Moreover, academic performance and self-confidence among the enrolled girls have shown marked improvement.

Despite these achievements, KGBVs continue to face several challenges. Infrastructural inadequacies, poor quality of education, and a general lack of awareness about the scheme hinder its effectiveness. Issues such as teacher absenteeism and insufficient staff training further exacerbate the problem. Additionally, many schools have limited access to technology and digital learning resources, which affects the overall quality of education offered.

Maulana Azad National Foundation

The Maulana Azad National Foundation was established with the primary objective of promoting education, cultural development, and social welfare among minority communities in India. The foundation plays a key role in empowering marginalized sections by offering scholarships to deserving minority students, thereby improving their access to quality education. It also provides support to various educational institutions and programs that cater to the needs of minority groups.

In addition to educational support, the foundation actively promotes cultural activities and exchange programs to foster mutual understanding and celebrate India's rich cultural diversity. Its initiatives focus on empowerment and inclusivity, aiming to integrate minority communities more fully into the national development framework. Over the years, the foundation has made significant contributions by enhancing educational opportunities and fostering cultural development within minority communities. It has helped increase access to education and opened up new avenues for personal and professional growth among students from underrepresented groups. The foundation has also been instrumental in promoting cultural diversity and exchange, strengthening the social fabric of the nation. However, the foundation faces certain challenges, including limited resources and funding, which constrain the scale and reach of its programs. There is also a need for more widespread awareness and outreach to ensure that the benefits of its initiatives reach all eligible beneficiaries.

Madrassas

Madrassas serve as traditional Islamic educational institutions with the primary objective of providing religious instruction and promoting cultural development within the Muslim community. These institutions focus on Islamic studies, including the Quran, Hadith, and Fiqh, as well as the Arabic language and classical Islamic literature. A strong emphasis is placed on moral values, discipline, and character formation, with the aim of nurturing spiritually aware and ethically grounded individuals. Madrassas also play a crucial role in preserving Islamic heritage and transmitting cultural and religious knowledge across generations.

Despite their historical and cultural significance, madrassas face several challenges. Many of them have a limited focus on contemporary subjects such as science, mathematics, and technology, which affects students' readiness for modern careers. Additionally, there is a perception that madrassas operate separately from the mainstream education system, which can lead to social and educational exclusion. The need for integration with the broader education framework and enhancement of the curriculum with modern subjects is increasingly recognized.

Nevertheless, madrassas hold considerable potential as educational institutions, especially in reaching marginalized communities that may lack access to formal schooling. By incorporating modern subjects and pedagogical practices while retaining their religious and cultural essence, madrassas can become inclusive centres of learning. Moreover, they offer a unique opportunity to promote interfaith dialogue, cultural understanding, and national integration through education.

CONCLUSION

The evaluation of centrally sponsored schemes for the education of SCs, STs, girls, and minorities reveals both significant progress and persistent challenges. These schemes have expanded access to education for millions of marginalized students through scholarships, residential schools, free uniforms and books, and mid-day meals. However, gaps remain in effective implementation, outreach, and monitoring, especially in remote and socio-economically backward regions where awareness and infrastructure are lacking.Status studies highlight improvements in enrolment and retention rates among SCs, STs, girls, and minorities over the past decades, indicating a positive shift in attitudes toward education. Nevertheless, these studies also expose regional disparities, gender-based dropouts, and quality issues. Learning outcomes for marginalized groups often remain below national averages, signaling the need for targeted academic support, language-appropriate materials, and better-trained teachers.Teaching-learning practices are critical in shaping inclusive classrooms. While policies increasingly emphasize equity and child-centric pedagogy, many schools still struggle to implement inclusive strategies effectively. Teachers often lack adequate training to handle diversity in the classroom, leading to exclusionary practices that hinder the participation and performance of children from marginalized backgrounds.

Social inclusion in education requires more than just physical access to schools. It involves creating a learning environment where all students feel safe, respected, and capable of achieving their potential. A shift towards culturally relevant pedagogy, multi-lingual education, and participatory learning approaches is necessary. This calls for consistent investment in teacher education, curriculum reform, and community involvement. Innovative institutional models like Navodaya Vidyalaya Samithi (NVS) demonstrate how inclusive excellence can be achieved. By offering quality education through residential schools to rural and underprivileged children, NVS provides an equal platform for academic and personal growth. Its transparent admission process and inclusive design have helped reduce educational disparities among rural youth.The Kasturba Gandhi Balika Vidyalaya (KGBV) scheme has been particularly impactful in addressing the educational needs of girls from disadvantaged communities. By providing safe, residential schooling along with academic and life skills support, KGBVs have played a key role in reducing gender gaps in upper primary education and empowering adolescent girls.

Institutions like the Maulana Azad National Foundation have supported minority education through scholarships, skill development programs, and awareness initiatives. Such targeted interventions help reduce dropout rates among minority students and encourage greater participation in higher education and employment. They also strengthen community trust in formal education systems.Traditional Madrassas, when integrated with mainstream education, offer a valuable model of culturally rooted and inclusive learning. In some states, modernized Madrassas now incorporate subjects like math, science, and language alongside religious teachings, helping students gain broader skills and opportunities. This hybrid model helps preserve cultural identity while promoting socio-economic mobility.Despite the progress made, a holistic approach is needed to ensure educational equity. This includes coordination between government departments, greater involvement of civil society, data-driven policy planning, and robust monitoring systems. Addressing social prejudices and infrastructural bottlenecks is crucial to achieving the vision of inclusive and quality education for all.

In conclusion, the education of SCs, STs, girls, minorities, and other marginalized groups has seen considerable policy attention and innovation. Yet, true inclusion will require sustained commitment, adaptive strategies, and continuous dialogue among stakeholders. Education must not only be accessible but also empowering, enabling every child to contribute meaningfully to society and lead a life of dignity and opportunity.

KEY POINTS

- **Evaluation of Centrally Sponsored Schemes for Marginalized Education:** Centrally sponsored schemes such as scholarships, free textbooks, residential schools, and midday meals have improved access to education for SCs, STs, girls, and minorities. These initiatives aim to reduce dropouts, promote retention, and improve learning environments. However, challenges remain in implementation efficiency, awareness, and monitoring, especially in remote and underdeveloped areas.
- **Status Study of Education Among Marginalized Groups:** Studies show that while enrolment has increased for SCs, STs, girls, and minorities, learning outcomes and retention rates remain uneven across regions. Socio-economic barriers, gender bias, and caste-based discrimination continue to affect educational equity. Disparities in infrastructure and quality of instruction also impact the effectiveness of these initiatives.
- **Teaching-Learning Practices and Social Inclusion:** Inclusive teaching practices are crucial for supporting diverse learners. While

policies promote equity and child-centred approaches, many classrooms still reflect traditional, exclusionary methods.

- Teachers often lack training in inclusive education, and there is a need for curriculum reforms and pedagogy that reflect the cultural and linguistic diversity of students.
- **Social Inclusion in Education:** Social inclusion goes beyond physical access to schools—it involves creating a respectful, safe, and supportive learning environment for all students. Inclusive education requires community involvement, teacher sensitization, multilingual materials, and culturally responsive teaching strategies to ensure no child feels marginalized or alienated.
- **Navodaya Vidyalaya Samithi (NVS):** NVS is a successful model of inclusive, high-quality residential education for talented rural students, including SCs, STs, and girls. With transparent admissions and government support, it provides a level playing field and promotes social integration, academic excellence, and leadership skills.
- **Kasturba Gandhi Balika Vidyalaya (KGBV):** KGBVs focus on the education of disadvantaged adolescent girls through residential schooling. These institutions address social and economic barriers by offering safety, basic amenities, and life skills training, which enhance enrolment, retention, and empowerment of girls from marginalized backgrounds.
- **Maulana Azad National Foundation:** This foundation supports minority education through scholarships, awareness drives, and development programs. Its interventions help bridge educational gaps for Muslim students, especially girls, and promote their participation in mainstream education and socio-economic development.
- **Madrassas and Modern Education Integration:** Madrassas, traditionally focused on religious education, are increasingly incorporating mainstream subjects like math, science, and languages. This integration offers minority students broader opportunities while preserving cultural identity, thus fostering inclusive growth and employability.
- **Need for Holistic Approaches:** Addressing educational inequality requires a multi-stakeholder approach involving government, educators, communities, and NGOs. Enhanced coordination, policy reforms, teacher training, and data-driven strategies are essential to make inclusion more effective and widespread.

Though significant progress has been made, sustained efforts are needed to ensure equity and quality in education for SCs, STs, girls, minorities, and other marginalized groups. Inclusive education must become the foundation of national development, empowering every learner to reach their full potential.

REFERENCES

1. Ambedkar, B.R. (n.d.). *Dr. B.R. Ambedkar and the upliftment of Marginalized Communities*. Only IAS. https://pwonlyias.com/upsc-notes/dr-ambedkar-marginalized-communities/
2. Cambridge University Press. (n.d.). Marginalization. In *Cambridge English Dictionary*. Retrieved May 4, 2025, from https://dictionary.cambridge.org/us/dictionary/english/marginalization
3. CultureAlly. (2025, April). *What does Marginalized mean and why does it matter?*https://www.cultureally.com/blog/what-does-marginalized-mean-and-why-does-it-matter
4. Freire, P. (2000). *Pedagogy of the Oppressed*. Continuum. https://envs.ucsc.edu/internships/internship-readings/freire-pedagogy-of-the-oppressed.pdf
5. Human Rights Watch. (2001). *Caste Discrimination: A Global Concern*. https://www.hrw.org/reports/pdfs/g/general/caste0801.pdf
6. Internet Encyclopaedia of Philosophy. (n.d.). Paulo Freire. Retrieved May 4, 2025, from https://iep.utm.edu/freire/
7. Kumar, K., & Sarangapani, P. (2018). Inclusive Education in India: Policy, Practice, and Challenges. *Indian Journal of Educational Studies*, 55(2), 45-60.
8. Mahatma Gandhi University. (n.d.). *Education of the Marginalized*. https://assist.mgu.ac.in/filemanager/assets/storage/DOC-CR1SE39NO1620.pdf
9. Mahila Samakhya Programme. (n.d.). *Empowering Women through Education*. Ministry of Education, Government of India. https://www.education.gov.in/en/mahila-samakhya-programme
10. Maulana Azad Education Foundation. (n.d.). *Begum Hazrat Mahal National Scholarship*. https://maef.nic.in
11. Merriam-Webster. (2025). Marginalize. In *Merriam-Webster.com dictionary*. Retrieved May 4, 2025, from https://www.merriam-webster.com/dictionary/marginalize
12. Ministry of Education. (2020). *National Education Policy 2020*. Government of India. https://www.education.gov.in
13. Ministry of Education. (2022). *Annual report 2021–22*. Government of India. https://www.education.gov.in
14. Ministry of Education. (2023). *Educational Statistics at a Glance*. Government of India. https://www.education.gov.in
15. Ministry of Education. (2023). *Samagra Shiksha – Kasturba Gandhi Balika Vidyalaya (KGBV)*. Government of India. https://www.education.gov.in/samagra-shiksha

16. Ministry of Human Resource Development. (1986). *National Policy on Education 1986*. Government of India. https://www.education.gov.in/sites/upload_files/mhrd/files/upload_document/npe.pdf
17. Ministry of Human Resource Development. (1992). *Programme of Action 1992*. Government of India. https://www.education.gov.in/sites/upload_files/mhrd/files/upload_document/POA.pdf
18. Ministry of Human Resource Development. (2005). *National Curriculum Framework 2005*. Government of India. https://ncert.nic.in/pdf/nc-framework/nf2005-english.pdf
19. Ministry of Minority Affairs. (2022). *Annual Report 2021–22*. Government of India. https://minorityaffairs.gov.in
20. Ministry of Minority Affairs. (2022). *Educational Empowerment of Minorities*. Government of India. https://minorityaffairs.gov.in
21. Ministry of Minority Affairs. (2022). *Schemes and Programmes*. Government of India. https://minorityaffairs.gov.in
22. Ministry of Minority Affairs. (2006). *Sachar Committee Report*. Government of India. https://minorityaffairs.gov.in/sites/default/files/sachar_comm.pdf
23. Ministry of Social Justice and Empowerment. (2022). *Annual Report 2021-22*. Government of India. https://socialjustice.gov.in
24. Ministry of Social Justice and Empowerment. (2022). *Post Matric Scholarship Scheme for SC Students*. Government of India. https://socialjustice.gov.in
25. Ministry of Social Justice and Empowerment. (1976). *Protection of Civil Rights Act, 1955 (amended in 1976)*. Government of India. https://legislative.gov.in/sites/default/files/A1955-22.pdf
26. Ministry of Social Justice and Empowerment. (1989). *Scheduled Castes and Scheduled Tribes (Prevention of Atrocities) Act, 1989*. Government of India. https://legislative.gov.in/sites/default/files/A1989-33.pdf
27. Ministry of Social Justice and Empowerment. (1995). *Persons with Disabilities (Equal Opportunities, Protection of Rights and Full Participation) Act, 1995*. Government of India. https://legislative.gov.in/sites/default/files/A1995-1.pdf
28. Ministry of Social Justice and Empowerment. (2016). *Rights of Persons with Disabilities Act, 2016*. Government of India. https://legislative.gov.in/sites/default/files/A2016-49_1.pdf
29. Ministry of Tribal Affairs. (2022). *Pre and Post Matric Scholarship Schemes for ST students*. Government of India. https://tribal.nic.in
30. Ministry of Tribal Affairs. (2022). *Statistical Profile of Scheduled Tribes in India 2022*. Government of India. https://tribal.nic.in
31. Ministry of Women and Child Development. (n.d.). *Kishori Shakti Yojana*. Government of India. https://wcd.nic.in/schemes/kishori-shakti-yojana
32. Ministry of Women and Child Development. (n.d.). *Rajiv Gandhi Scheme for Empowerment of Adolescent Girls (SABLA)*. Government of India. https://wcd.nic.in/schemes/rajiv-gandhi-scheme-empowerment-adolescent-girls-sabla

33. National Commission for Scheduled Castes. (2000). *Report on the Status of Scheduled Castes and Scheduled Tribes in India*. https://ncsc.nic.in/files/ncsc/new4/Annual_Report_2000.pdf
34. National Council of Educational Research and Training. (2021). *Inclusive Education for Children with Special needs*. https://ncert.nic.in
35. National Council of Educational Research and Training. (2022). *Status of Education among Disadvantaged Groups in India*. NCERT Publications.
36. National Institute of Educational Planning and Administration. (2021). *Evaluation of Centrally Sponsored Schemes for Education of Disadvantaged Groups*. NIEPA Publications.
37. National Institute of Educational Planning and Administration. (2021). *Innovations in School Education: Case studies from India*. https://www.niepa.ac.in
38. Navodaya Vidyalaya Samiti. (n.d.). *About NVS*. https://navodaya.gov.in/nvs/en/About-us/
39. Observer Research Foundation. (2020, July 30). *Equitable and Inclusive Vision in the National Educational Policy 2020*. https://www.orfonline.org/expert-speak/equitable-and-inclusive-vision-in-the-nep-2020
40. Office of the High Commissioner for Human Rights. (n.d.). *About Minorities and Human Rights*. Retrieved May 4, 2025, from https://www.ohchr.org/en/minorities/about-minorities-and-human-rights
41. Right to Education Initiative. (2000). *The Dakar Framework for Action: Education for All: Meeting our Collective Commitments*. https://www.right-to-education.org/resource/dakar-framework-action
42. Singal, N. (2019). Challenges and Opportunities in Implementing Inclusive Education in India. *International Journal of Inclusive Education*, 23(12), 1249-1263. https://doi.org/10.1080/13603116.2018.1460691
43. Swami Vivekananda. (n.d.). *The Saint and the Subaltern: How Swami Vivekananda became the Voice for the Marginalized Communities*. MediaLit. https://medialit.in/thevoices/saint-and-the-sub-altern-how-swami-vivekananda-became-the-voice-for-the-marginalised-communities/
44. UNESCO. (2020). *Education and Inclusion*. https://unesco.org/themes/inclusion-in-education
45. UNESCO. (2020). *Global Education Monitoring Report: Inclusion and Education – All means all*. https://unesdoc.unesco.org
46. United Nations. (2000). *United Nations Millennium Declaration*. https://www.un.org/millennium/declaration/ares552e.htm
47. United Nations. (2015). *Transforming our World: The 2030 Agenda for Sustainable Development*. https://sdgs.un.org/2030agenda
48. United Nations Development Programme. (n.d.). *Sustainable Development Goals*. Retrieved May 4, 2025, from https://www.undp.org/sustainable-development-goals

49. United Nations Educational, Scientific and Cultural Organization. (2000). *The Dakar Framework for Action: Education for All: Meeting our Collective Commitments.* https://unesdoc.unesco.org/ark:/48223/pf0000121147
50. United Nations International Children's Emergency Fund. (n.d.). *Early Childhood Development.* Retrieved May 4, 2025, from https://www.unicef.org/early-childhood-development
51. UNICEF India. (2021). *Equity and Inclusion in Education in India.* https://www.unicef.org/india
52. UNICEF India. (2021). *Learning for Every Child: Bridging the Inclusion Gap.* https://www.unicef.org/india
53. UNICEF India. (2021). *Promoting Education among Marginalized Children.* https://www.unicef.org/india
54. Wikipedia Contributors. (n.d.). *Millennium Development Goals.* In *Wikipedia, The Free Encyclopaedia.* Retrieved May 4, 2025, from https://en.wikipedia.org/wiki/Millennium_Development_Goals

Index